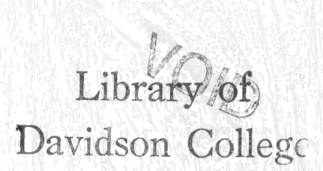

ESSAYS
WRITTEN IN PRAISE
OF PUBLIC LIBRARIES

The Library Connection

compiled by the

PUBLIC LIBRARY ASSOCIATION

a division of the

AMERICAN LIBRARY ASSOCIATION

AMERICAN LIBRARY ASSOCIATION

Chicago 1977

Library of Congress Cataloging in Publication Data
Main entry under title:

The Library connection.
1. Public libraries—United States—Addresses, essays, lectures. I. Public Library Association.
Z731.L57 027.4′73 77-24687
ISBN 0-8389-0245-6

Printed in the United States of America

Contents

Contents

Introduction

Many people do not realize the potential of the public library to enrich the lives of members of a community. Several years ago the Public Library Association (PLA) concluded that one way to overcome this lack of understanding would be to publish a book which shows in vivid terms how public libraries have been and can be used by individuals. With the financial assistance of the Council on Library Resources, PLA was able to commission personal essays by a number of well-known people describing how libraries have played a role in their own lives and could play a similar role in the lives of others. Each essay would be directed to a specific audience—the aged, consumers, homeowners, and many others. These essays, some of which have already been published in periodicals, are for the benefit of other citizens who may not know what public libraries can do for them.

The articles which follow are full of testimonials from an assortment of satisfied consumers of the services of the American public library—artists like Ezra Jack Keats, writers like Nat Hentoff, people in business, homemakers, parents. These are people who know that the public library system, extending into nearly every corner of the United States, is undoubtedly our country's most valuable intellectual, cultural, and recreational resource—and perhaps also its most underexploited and underappreciated. These are wise consumers—taxpayers who realize that it is their dollars that make this unique resource a reality and are determined to get every penny's worth and more.

Some came late to this knowledge—like retired bookseller and editor Lavinia Russ, who confesses that for the first seventy years of her life, she studiously avoided libraries until, "I went to the Brooklyn Public Library, and even before I went through its wide doors, I began to discover how poor and narrow my life had been." Some learned about libraries much earlier—like writer Sol Yurick, who used libraries to resist the public school system's stranglehold on his imagination and intellect: "Reading books, non-assigned books, prevented you from becoming rigid . . . the library saved me, was my real education." The adult creations of many of the more famous contributors to this handbook were sparked by what they learned—about themselves and their world—at the library as children.

Libraries are not in the business of making a profit, but they are very much in the business of serving people. Indeed, their very existence depends on the support and use of many individuals. Since what libraries have to offer can truly enhance and change lives, becoming an informed library consumer is not a luxury reserved for people with time to kill. It is a necessity. PLA hopes that this book will encourage people to use their public libraries and will thus be instrumental in enriching both their lives and the lives of the libraries which serve them.

Jacob K. Javits

FOREWORD

The public library is one of America's greatest institutions. Open to every person who has the curiosity to go inside, the library can be an extremely useful tool in helping us to make sense of what is going on around us on a local, national, and international level. Through a study of history, we can begin to understand how we have arrived at the present, and through careful monitoring of the present, we can all help to shape the future.

Most of us first became acquainted with libraries at school, but thanks to our public library system, leaving school or finishing college does not have to mark the end of our education. I have always found that curiosity generates more curiosity, that finding out the answer to one question invariably leads to other questions, other answers, and ultimately to a well-informed outlook on the world. Few people would argue with the fact that a well-informed citizen is a better citizen, one who can contribute in a very real way to the process of government.

As a young boy in New York's lower East Side, I was taught the value of reading by my mother, who could then (she learned at age fifty-five) neither read nor write English. She encouraged me then, and later on, to read as many books as I could get my hands on. My family was much too poor to afford the luxury of buying books, so our local public library was invaluable, an essential part of my growing and learning years, and I read voraciously: history, philosophy, biography, essays of criticism, novels, and short stories.

History was my major interest, and I remember my own excitement as I discovered that our system of government had its roots so deep in the past, in the civilization of the ancient Greeks, the thinkers who were responsible for evolving the concept of democracy (itself a Greek word meaning government of the people). Also the challenge to my conscience as I learned that these innovative ancient Greeks, while believing in the idea of a government of the people, did not include slaves in the category of "people." Slaves were imported from abroad, usually captives of foreign wars, and to the Greeks anyone who was not a Greek did not qualify as a human being, and was therefore not entitled to vote.

The history of our own country, itself born of a revolution against a normally enlightened nation, is a stirring and brilliant tribute to man's search for dignity and social justice. Particularly in view of the recent Bicentennial celebrations, America's past makes a richly rewarding study. Most public libraries have extensive material on this history, and through it we can discover that even in America, the democratic system has taken a long time to perfect, with the vote being given only gradually to people without property, to women, and, much later still, really assured to blacks.

Our public libraries can also help to remind us of our origins, an invaluable service to Americans as we are all products of the melting pot. As generations pass, and the memories of our immigrant ancestors recede, it begins to require a positive effort not to lose touch with our plural ethnic and cultural backgrounds. Most libraries, particularly local ones, will have a selection of books on the history and culture of the countries that our parents and grandparents left to seek their fortunes in the New World. Although many of our communities retain their ethnic characters, and although traditions are faithfully followed year after year, the original meanings of these traditions are often lost in time. Reading from the library shelves can make the beginnings of ethnic communities both instructive and romantic, like newly discovered worlds. Such knowledge gives us growth as Americans and enriches the fabric of our nation.

But it is not only by making it possible for us to read history that libraries can be of service. What affects us most directly is the present. As voters, we are all responsible for ensuring that the representatives we feel best reflect the quality of our nation and our views are elected. We can use the resources of the library to learn the issues against which to measure the opinions of the candidates, to find out where they really stand politically. Most libraries keep back issues of local and national newspapers and magazines. There are any number of reference books to assist in locating speeches made by candidates, and the genuinely curious reader can even request back numbers of the *Congressional Record* to check on the voting records of candidates who are already incumbents.

I suspect that many people feel that they cannot rival the experts, and that decisions regarding, for example, the energy crisis or foreign policy, are better left to the experts and to the politicians who work at it and are therefore better qualified to make decisions. But this is giving up too soon and, thanks to the resources of our public libraries, people who have the time and the inclination to look into these matters will find that most of the information that their representatives are privy to is also available to them. In this way, library users with initiative can not only make their own decisions, but they can also understand more fully the decisions made by their local and state legislators, their congressman, their senators, their governor, and the president. If one disagrees with his or her representative, one then has the tools at hand (the information) to question these decisions, and to affect future ones. Many people do not realize how important the opinions of their constituents are to public officials. In many instances, a letter from a well-informed constituent will shed new light, or simply approach from a different angle a problem that may have become routinized to the representative through over-familiarity. Such a letter may also draw attention to a new problem or case of injustice.

I cannot emphasize strongly enough the value of public libraries to the public and to those of us in public life. And it is of course true that the more a library is used, the more it will grow, and the more useful it will become, and the more it will be used—and so on in a never ending upward spiral of growth for the library, and ever-increasing reward and pleasure for the user.

Marchette Chute

AN OPEN DOOR

We wish many things for our children. Above all we wish them liberty, the right to live their lives freely with no doors slammed in their faces. We want them to be able to move wherever their hearts and their minds take them. We want no path closed to them because they may be poor, or belong to the "wrong" sex, or have the "wrong" color—all those savage and irrational constrictions that have so injured and impoverished the human race. The turmoil of the twentieth century has been in part the result of a fierce determination to achieve this liberty for everyone, so that no child of the future would be forced to suffer what the children of the past have endured.

Yet there is another kind of limitation, and one that is self-imposed. It is possible to encounter an open door and walk past as though it were closed. There is treasure inside, but it will be useless as long as it is unused.

There are many such doors, but the one I am thinking of in particular belongs to that blessed institution, the public library.

Centuries ago this would have been a contradiction in terms, for a library was a private thing, not a public one. Rich men could afford a few hundred volumes, but they would lend them only to their close friends. Churches and colleges could acquire larger collections, but they always restricted them to their own members, and even so the authorities felt it was desirable that some of the books should be chained.

What was once private and exclusive is now public, available to anyone who wants it. And yet, though the treasure is open and unguarded, there are many people who walk unseeing past the open library door. They give their children "everything," as they say, but it never occurs to them to take the hand of the child and walk in.

One reason for this is obvious. A small child can listen to a symphony by Mozart and be delighted, or look at a portrait by Renoir and understand very well what the painter intended. But a book is only a bound set of hieroglyphics on white paper until the child has learned to read, and, even so, there is usually a period of struggle before the youngster acquires the easy familiarity with the printed page that transforms it into a pathway to pleasure.

It is true that some children make friends with books instantly. They learn to read before anyone has a chance to teach them, and for the rest of their lives they possess a source of endless horizons and unfailing delight. It is no problem to lure children like these to a public library. The problem rather is to persuade them to leave, and when they do they will be staggering triumphantly under a splendid pile of those indispensable items to which their library cards have entitled them.

It is also true that some children find it almost impossible to make friends with books. Faced with those black marks on the white paper, they embark upon a process so slow and so laborious that they naturally avoid the act of reading as much as they can. I feel a special sympathy for such children, for I have the same relationship to mathematics. In spite of the industry of my youth and the even greater industry of my teachers, I still tend to count on my fingers and I am not at all clear about percentages. I never rose above a primitive and hostile relationship to mathematics because I never saw the necessity. I notice, however, that I can add up a grocery bill quickly and accurately; and even the most reluctant young reader, suddenly needing to know what a book is saying, is quite capable of showing a similar skill.

Between these two kinds of readers, the ardent and the reluctant, are the majority of children. To them the printed word is neither a friend nor an enemy. They know what the words on the page mean and can turn to them for information or entertainment. But, like skiers who slide cautiously down very small slopes, they never move on to the dazzle and excitement of the real thing. They know the technique of reading, but they do not know the art.

The art of reading, like the art of skiing, is acquired by doing so much of it that it becomes natural. The skier achieves this by having hills and snow available to him. The reader does it by having books.

This is where the public library emerges in all its glory. It offers many things nowadays—films, exhibits, recordings, even games that can be borrowed from the desk. But, above all, it offers books. It offers them with a lavishness which not even very rich fathers and mothers could afford for their children and of which most parents could not even dream.

Moreover, the books are offered without supervision, setting free that wonderful, flexible instrument—the attention of the child—to roam in a land without boundaries. Some children will stay with picture books for a long time, or will remember something that a librarian shared in a story hour and rejoice to find it suddenly on the printed page. Others (or the same children in a bolder mood) will take down more complicated books from the shelves and stumble through them adventurously, confused but happy, with no one to ask them what they think they are doing or why they are doing it. Some small researcher may wish to concentrate on dinosaurs and retreat raptly into their special world, surrounded by all the available books on the subject and thinking private thoughts that possibly only a fellow dinosaur could understand. From Shakespeare to Peter Rabbit and back again, the children inside a public library are free to read in any way they wish, and there will be enough for everyone.

It is in this way that they enter into the art of reading. There are other ways it can be achieved but it happens most easily in a public library, where thousands of books are waiting for small, exploring hands and lively, astonished minds. The treasure is there for the asking, transforming the children into increasingly delighted travelers in a world that expands every time they enter it.

The first step is the important one, the first movement across the threshold and through the open door. The children will do the rest for themselves, and the more they read the more they will enjoy reading. But it is an adult who supplies the introduction, and this is usually the child's own father or mother.

Some parents can hardly wait to share this kingdom with their children and have no problem at all. But some feel shy where books are concerned, and what looks like indifference is really a feeling of uncertainty. It might help such parents to be less self-conscious if they were to realize what the library shelves are really offering.

In nineteenth-century England there were many laboring children, and they were not permitted to learn their letters. This was an official policy, so that they would always remain locked into a low station in life. In parts of America, in the same century, it was a criminal offense to teach Negro children to read, and for the same reason. There was no surer way to condemn them to a life of subjection; they must never be given the skill that might set them free.

No child faces that now, and the hearts of fathers and mothers no longer break because their children remain bound in the brutal chains of illiteracy. But there are other, more slender cords that bind some children still and that prevent them from entering their full birthright of freedom. There are many ways of entering this birthright, but to possess the art of reading will always remain one of the most potent.

The fathers and mothers who know this are the ones who read to their babies, so that books are loved objects from the first. They are the ones who have books always available in the house, so that the written word is a familiar friend and never a formidable stranger. Such parents might even like to make a special occasion out of a child's first visit to the public library, a special ceremony out of the excitement of getting one's first library card.

For indeed it is a kind of birthday that is being celebrated, a milestone on the road to growing up.

Nat Hentoff

LIBRARIES: MAKING CONNECTIONS

When I was growing up in Roxbury (part of Boston), the nearest public library was twelve long blocks away. It was attached to a fortress-like high school and by contrast with the multifariously inviting contemporary libraries I've seen in Tulsa and Philadelphia, among other cities in recent years, our library was forbidding. The rule of silence was so zealously enforced that a Trappist monk could have stayed there for years without being tempted to break his vows. There was no audiovisual section, no booths for listening to recordings, no recordings. The librarians were efficient but hardly outgoing, not at all like what I consider to be the new breed of librarian during the past fifteen years or so—these quite remarkably cheerful people who appear to like what they do for a living more than most people do.

Nonetheless, I looked forward to my Saturday library visits almost as much as I did to the Saturday afternoon picture show, the nearly four-hour-long cornucopia every week of a double feature, strings of shorts and previews, and the literally cliff-hanging serials. The library too was a cornucopia, and I never ceased marveling at the continual surprises that came with a library card. And unlike school, one could find and keep on finding one's own surprises.

Nobody, for instance, had told me when I was eight about the Andrew Lang books of fairy tales—the *Red Book* and the *Blue Book* and all those other colors. But I found them, and I read them all. Then I found the sea tales of Howard Pease and all kinds of novels that could never have been on my reading lists at school because they were too old for me. But only I knew what was too old for me. I sometimes wonder if I wouldn't know a lot more by now if I had simply stayed in the library during those years and not gone to school at all. It is, after all, an education prescription that George Bernard Shaw recommended for children and I wish that instead of leaving a large sum of money for work on simplifying the English language, Shaw had instead left bequests for researchers to test whether kids growing up in libraries rather than in classrooms become smarter and more self-confident than their peers hooked to their desks.

Anyway, as the years went on, I kept making new discoveries in the library—collections of old newspapers which gave me my first sense of the excitement of reading about history as it was turning into history. And magazines. All kinds of magazines new and old in all kinds of fields, many of them fascinatingly arcane. And I would have known about hardly any of them had it not been for the library.

I became such a library freak that I could be perfectly content for an hour just going through the card catalog, coming upon the titles of books I simply had to read, delighted that they were there, waiting. To this day, I cannot leave a library without spending some browsing time at the card catalog. Actually, it's not all browsing. I invariably search out the cards for my own books because only their inclusion in a library makes me feel like an authentic author. Seeing them in a book store window is not nearly so satisfying.

Admittedly, libraries have improved a great deal since my boyhood although, in retrospect, I have no complaint about ours except the rule that kids could only take out kids' books. (With the help of an occasionally subversive librarian, I used to break that rule, enjoying the forbidden book all the more, but I thought it was a silly rule, and I still think so.) Whatever a kid thinks he might want to read, he ought to have a shot at. I remember when I was eleven conniving to take home a huge, scholarly, critical work on Lenin. I don't know why I was interested in Lenin at eleven, but although I couldn't understand most of the book I felt very proud of getting through as much of it as I did. That journey stretched my vocabulary; led me later to approach Edmund Wilson's *To the Finland Station* with the supportive sense that I had some background in the subject; and, all in all, made me feel like a very competent eleven-year-old boy. And that, obviously, is a good way for an eleven-year-old boy to feel.

As I was saying though, libraries have evolved since then in diversely intriguing ways. One of my daughters, for instance, is a musician, and at the Lincoln Center Library in New York City she has greatly supplemented what she's learned in school and from her piano teacher. Not only through books but through scores and recordings. Another daughter, though nominally in college, is a circus performer (clown, juggler, fire-eater), and she tells me that at various libraries she's visited, she's been able to find more about circus lore than in her university library (the university, misguidedly, does not regard circus history as a "serious" enough branch of learning to collect books on the subject).

It is that quality—the democracy of the library—which seems to me to have deepened and broadened in the years since I first started those Saturday morning trips to our library. Because, I suppose, librarians are now themselves more heterogeneous in their backgrounds and experiences, an extraordinarily wide range of interests can be filled, if not satiated, at most libraries. I was a baseball nut, for instance, as a kid, but there were precious few books on baseball in our library. Not so now. You can major in baseball at some libraries.

In one sense, some of the kids I know are using the library in a way we did but with more resources to work with. When you're in school, you don't get much real information on what options you might have when you grow up. I know, there's an increasing amount of "career choice" discussion in some schools, but most of it is pretty shallow and abstract. It's much more fun and more instructive to read about people who have done some of the things a kid thinks he might want to do. If the biographies are accurately detailed and well-written (and adult biographies, I urge again, ought to be available to kids), it is possible to get a palpable sense of what a life in the law is like, or in psychiatry, or in politics, or in running a zoo, for that matter.

Furthermore, there are resourceful teachers who are suggesting to kids that they can get a more palpable sense of the past by comparing what current history books have to say about a particular period with what newspapers and magazines of that time were saying. Once hooked on that kind of library research it's difficult to keep insisting that history is such a boring subject. A while ago, my thirteen-year-old elder son got so excited reading a *Harper's Weekly* editorial lacerating President Andrew Johnson that he came shouting into our room—the only time since the resignation of Richard Nixon that he has shown so intensely kinetic a reaction to the news. And that 1866 *Harper's Weekly* editorial did hit him as *news*. What better way to learn history?

It works the other way around too. Kids have told me of librarians who hold current events sessions. Not the old-style current events presentations which are usually numbing extensions of the already boring enough format show-and-tell. These new explorations in the library, on the other hand, get started from what the kids have seen on television or read in the papers and are then expanded to connect with books or films on the subject and with ways of relating it to similar events in the past. All this is done analytically—questioning the reporters' sources, examining the use of language (was it loaded?), figuring out the historians' sources (and how "objective" *were* they?).

What a library's present resources lead to is a style of learning, or rather styles of learning, that can thrive on the most natural approach to finding out what you want to know about all kinds of things. And that way is making connections. From books to films to recordings to newspapers to magazines to prints to telephone hookups to people who can tell you more of what you want to know. A number of libraries in recent years have set up that kind of hookup with me in fields I write about, from education to music to books for children. For an hour or more, I answer questions from youngsters and ask them a few. Also, libraries are getting a rising number of guests to come in and talk; and since libraries cover everything, there's no limit to the kinds of guests they can invite.

By and large, there's more active learning going on in libraries these days than in most other places in this society. And my sense of the matter is that as more and more connections are needed, libraries are going to continue being even more stimulating energy sources. It's too bad politicians don't spend more time in them.

Ezra Jack Keats

MEMORIES OF THE ARTIST AS A BOY

I was delivered to the library by the most unlikely circumstances—all of them unrelated to books.

We lived in a rundown tenement in the East New York section of Brooklyn, where I attended junior high school during the depression. After finishing my homework, I ran the household errands—to the accompaniment of abuse from the shopkeepers about our unpaid bills.

"Yeah, I know—your father still ain't workin'. Tell him I'm a poor man too—a few more days an' no more credit! We ain't givin' dis stuff away."

Diminished and humiliated, I returned with the barest necessities, plus messages I found painful to deliver. The house was leaden with defeat. It was a bitter and unhappy marriage—the triumph of a matchmaker whose immigrant victims must have been legion. "Oh, God, what's the use? What's the use?" was my mother's depressing incantation.

So I'd hole up and draw—I copied pictures of fancy ladies on magazine covers, and newspaper photos of airplanes, dirigibles, famous actors and gangsters, scenes from my window—and an occasional graveyard. Or I'd take long walks—anywhere, I thought—so long as it was away from home. But like a somnambulist, I headed toward the part of town where a certain girl, Harriet Tawarski, lived. I had a crush on her. Sometimes she was standing on the sagging porch of her grey, unpainted house as I passed, my heart beating like mad. She waved to me and turned my legs into accordions. I managed to walk by and wave back. I told myself, "So what?" I didn't pass there just to see *her*, and staggered on.

One day, my adrenalin (or whatever it was) raced through me as Harriet waved and I was propelled onward block after block and found myself on another planet. It was lined with quiet lanes of huge gnarled trees, lush lawns, behind which rose silent symbols of what struck me as an untroubled world—big, well kept, imposing houses, surrounded by perfectly trimmed shrubbery. I peered from behind white fences through the windows. Nothing stirred. I don't recall seeing anyone entering or leaving. Didn't they work—or go shopping? I passed silently through dappled shade cast by ancient trees whose huge trunks sent twisted roots deep into the green earth. I became addicted to those trips, discovering new avenues of peace and enchantment.

A few days later I found myself standing in front of a building quite different from the others. It had nice, even rows of red bricks, broad steps, tall pillars, and big doors. I thought it was a hospital. Looking up I saw "Brooklyn Public Library, Arlington Branch" carved in marble. I leaned against a tree and watched to see what went on there. A couple of girls tripped up the steps and went inside. Some people came out chatting amiably. Soon I found myself walking up the steps past the imposing pillars and going inside—into a hushed atmosphere that had an unfamiliar smell—books. Rows and rows of books, all around me. People sat at tables reading books and strange newspapers. Everywhere I turned I saw signs for different subjects—Science, Politics, History, Poetry. Books about everything. Facing me was a sign labelled Art. I reached up and picked a book at random. Egyptian art. The text was impossible to understand, but I was fascinated by the new words and pictures. Holding the book, I felt important. There were sections and sections of books on art. Greek, Italian, Chinese, Indian, English, French, African, American, Dutch. I wandered around and discovered that I could get a card, become a member of the library, and actually take these books home. I returned regularly and began to read the art books from one end of the shelf to the next. I didn't understand the language or references. I read, and gazed long at the reproductions. In the meantime, I carved from soap and wood, and painted with anything, even mercurochrome. A house painter across the street befriended me, and supplied me with leftover materials.

I continued reading. If anyone had asked me what I was reading I couldn't possibly have told him. Yet, today I remember grasping the essence of Egyptian sculpture in Wilenski's book. How deeply and affectionately his name is etched in my mind—together with John Ruskin and so many others.

Finally I reached the last of the art books. For some reason, the stacks ended with the advent of the Impressionists. I went away with the notion that Impressionism was the wave of the future. Little did I know that it was decades old, abandoned in the rapid development of modern art. I painted my version of Impressionism, and got the kids in the neighborhood who painted excited about it. "Ya see, these guys paint with little strokes of color, one next to the other. When you step back they all blend together. That way you get more vibrant color." A fancy word like "vibrant" impressed the hell out of them, and soon they were all Impressionists.

I hadn't any idea of what was happening then—learning and developing deep ties to a world of art through words I didn't understand and paintings I never saw.

There are times now, sometimes in foreign lands, standing before the original works of art, when those names and ideas magically surface—and I realize that I had understood, way back then.

This morning at about 4:00 A.M. I awoke and read what I had written here, and found myself possessed by an irresistible yearning to return to the library to see how time had treated it. Would it be there—surrounded by those lovely trees and houses? Well, there it was—

the same—a little worn, a little smaller—and closed. I walked up the stairs and rapped on the door. Someone signalled to me from inside—"We're closed." I had to get in there. I rapped again, harder and louder. The door opened a crack. I explained that I was writing an article about the library. "Could I come in?" The door opened and I was fourteen again. It was all there. The same shelves, books, electric fans, and those windows, the trees smack up against them, reaching in as if to grab me. They had the same power over me as when I was a boy. The view from the windows reminded me of the solace, the promise, the beauty they had always offered me. I looked around and saw a familiar stairway with "Reference Room" painted at the top. I walked up softly, afraid to break the spell. Here were the tables where I used to bring the big art books which you couldn't take home, excitingly filled with grand color reproductions. I'd take my place at the tables with stern, silent, studious adults, with my own pile of books, turning pages as each tipped-in picture revealed itself to me. Life welled up inside me. I would be an artist. How simple it all seemed then.

I retraced my steps to the main floor, and walked to the other end of the library. There I found an identical staircase. I could not recall ever having seen it before. I looked up at the sign—"Children's Room." Why hadn't I ever noticed it? By the time I began to use the library I may have considered myself long past children's books—as a matter of fact, in the world I came from, nobody seemed to know about them. Halfway up the steps I wondered, "Would they be there?" I hurried to the top and looked for the picture books. I scanned the shelves—there they were! I stood looking at my own books on the shelves and mused at the wonder of it all. What long and winding paths had taken me from that staircase to this one?

Sol Yurick

ON BEING POOR AND HAVING LIBRARIES

I grew up during the last depression. Ten years. From 1929 to 1939. Those were my formative years.

People usually think about poverty merely in terms of not having enough food, no money, the inability to move around. You're stuck in one neighborhood and there's no way out. Poor people have stunted visions as well as malnourished bodies. Vision isn't only fed by the things you see in the limited amount of space you can cover; it's also a question of inner space. Of course, if you're starving then the inner space collapses completely.

For me, and for most of the people I lived among, Jews mostly, books enabled one to endure, and finally were the key to the way out. It was part of our tradition, our cultural capital, our ancient heritage, our *social* genetics. We dreamed of being scientists, lawyers, doctors, dentists, accountants, lawmakers, social workers, of being writers and poets. And if these fields were cut off, many of us dreamed of revolution so we could create a system in which we could be those things. Among us were liberal reformers and conservatives, legalistic socialists and revolutionaries. At least that's what our parents were. One thing, whatever our political persuasion was, whether we were going to be hustlers or respectable, one thing we all agreed on: the book could show us the way out, the way to change ourselves and to change the structure of things. And, if as some revolutionaries assert, power comes out of a gun, the book tells you that you may need a gun, or for that matter who to point that gun at. Revolutionaries, at least left-wing revolutionaries, are also people of the book. Revolutionaries in those days felt they should know more about everything than anyone else: it was a rage for knowledge. Everything. This they taught to their children. Others who saw the need for change but were reformist in temperament had to know the way things worked in order to change them. And then, of course, there were those who could, through books, float in realms that the boundaries imposed by neighborhood and poverty could not contain. Knowledge was a kind of food that supplemented your diet and stopped, for a while, the pangs of hunger. Does that sound silly? If a harsh or loving word can instantly change your feelings in a way that can be measured by biometric instruments, then why won't a book allay your hunger—for a while? This, we, as Jews, had learned for over two thousand years and, to an extent, it had worked.

Schooling in those days was not so much neglectful as harsh, rigid, authoritarian, narrowly programmed, stifling of the imagination (unless you ran across a wonderful teacher—but that was rare). You read books in school in certain sequences and did a lot of learning through unimaginative methods. But after all, public education was education planned for an industrial society; and schools, for the lower classes, were set up to duplicate factories. You learned disciplined procedure through assembly-line methods. The hour was structured, the learning planned, imagination stopped at the border of an hour, the path to excellence led through a textbook written for the lowest common denominator.

Terror, fear of failure, and the search for the way up and out kept a lot of kids locked to their chairs, repeating endlessly things that didn't always make sense. Reading books, nonassigned books, prevented you from becoming rigid; it let you learn things out of sequence, read things that weren't prescribed, or were even proscribed, and even let you feel that you knew more than the teacher—which might well have been true. Once, I was caught reading Darwin's *Origin of Species* in sixth grade and was upbraided before the whole class. Whether it was because the book should have properly been read in college or because the teacher was anti-evolution, I never found out. In any case, Darwin, for me, in my grade, was as forbidden as pornography. But, since one did not challenge teachers then, the way out was to practice secrecy, resistance; if the school, or the teacher, didn't want me to read these books, these were the books I was going to read.

But, being poor, who could afford to buy books? We were getting "welfare," "home relief." There was no allowance for growth. Subsistence was all. But then, there was always the library. The library saved me, was my real education, my resistance, my secrecy.

The nearest library was about five miles away. (No, I remember that there was a public library much nearer, but it wasn't as big as the Fordham Branch. Somehow, bigness was a part of it. I still have dreams in which I wander into a secret immense library full of books I never heard about, books full of people and events and languages I never imagined. I pick up a book and begin to read and my head reels because the world here is put together in an entirely different way. "So that's the way it is," I say and am happy because I have a whole library of the unknown I'm going to find out about. Why was this library never known to me? And what's more, I'm going to understand in a different way everything I've read and done. And so part of it was to be able to walk into a huge room and see thousands of books, more than you could ever hope to read in a lifetime, a part of a way of satisfying this hunger for knowledge; more food than you can ever consume. Knowledge? That's too simple a term for it. I didn't merely seek fact, information, dates. I hungered for imagination itself: lean bodies, fat imaginations!) The trip to the library could be made by taking two trolleys. Or, by walking through Bronx Park, the whole five miles. And back. It sounds like one of those

Lincolnesque kinds of things, where the older person tells the younger what they had to suffer to get where they wanted to. I never thought of it that way at all. The trip was part of it. You deferred satisfaction and built up the desire and then the gratification was more intense.

In those days the library permitted only four books at a time. I would take the four books and walk, or ride home. When I got home I would open one, then another, trying to decide which one to begin with; the one that looked the most interesting? The one that seemed the least interesting, saving the best for last? And finally, deciding on one, lying on the bed would plunge into it and for a time the world around me would disappear and my mind would be gorged. I would have to be called for lunch or supper. I would come, carrying an open book, reading as I walked through two spaces, that of the book and that of our apartment. I would sit at the table through the eating, reading in spite of my mother's objections that reading would spoil my appetite. Who cared?

None of which is to say that I didn't do the things that other kids did. But on some days—reading can be a drug. Books can also produce dreams. People I know have become word-addicts; they drown in dreams. Books and the real world should interpenetrate.

Maybe it was even the nonstructured way in which I read which led, finally, to my being fascinated by everything possible. I would get out novels for a while and then grow bored. I would then wander to the science section and load up on books on biology and geology and physics and astronomy and read till I could take no more. Then it would be biography and mathematics, or even books on commercial history and then I would go back to novels again. The habit stays with me still. I remember in college when the time came for me to take an economics final, I managed to read all of Proust, something I couldn't do for literature courses.

Ultimately, this led to my beginning to feel as if everything in the world was in some way related to everything else and that the way in which we learned things, divided into disciplines and areas of studies, was a bad way to learn. And perhaps this was behind my decision, my drive, to become a writer. Of course I couldn't have explained it that way in those days. I just resisted discipline and discipline narrows the mind. I was just reacting in an instinctive and self-preservative way.

And of course, ultimately, though I couldn't have put it in words then, the key to any kind of success, admittance to the top of any field, lay in language itself and how you use it and how you penetrate other languages. Though I didn't know it, between the ages of ten and fifteen I followed the prescriptions of an elite education, which educates the language sense first. The specializations follow. The greatest minds, whether you talk about an Einstein, a Thomas Mann, a Proust, a Norbert Wiener, a Lenin, a Mao, or a Marx, began in this manner, ranging across the whole field of thought and had this primary concern with language. Well, wasn't Mao a librarian for a while? And didn't Lenin title one of his most important works, *What Is To Be Done*, after a novel by Cherneshevsky; a novel which had burned its way into his imagination? And didn't Norbert Wiener dip into his knowledge of Greek to call his field cybernetics (after the Greek *steersman*)? And wasn't Marx enthralled by Goethe?

These were the things that made life livable for me in the middle of poverty, that enabled me to travel thousands of miles without moving a foot, that enabled me to understand the world I lived in and rooted me in a certain commonality of all humans.

Now there are two kinds of memory. One is personal and the other social, collective, or rather *collected*. The collected works of any political, economic, cultural, historical entity is a group memory and has just as much a role in the life of the personal mind (and its effect on action) as the memory of particular events in an individual's life. A memory is also a library. And one of the great wrongs the Crusaders visited on the Mohammedans was to take their knowledge, their memories, and libraries back to Europe. And one of the great wrongs one does oneself is to limit one's memory by not opening the self to a library.

Herman Badillo

LIBRARIES AND HISPANIC AMERICANS

There are very few government services left in our complex society that are not only locally supported by communities, but that also serve those communities' own needs directly and effectively. The library is one of these rare animals.

A pitiful paradox, however, exists in the situation of today's libraries. While these institutions have been changing their emphasis drastically in recent years—from mere book distributors to resource and information centers that handle every type of education media, their clientele has barely changed at all. The library has a mythical reputation for being a democratic institution —the haven of the self-made man. The ambitious worker, bent on self-improvement and climbing the steep ladder of success, could burn the night oil over the library books and use his or her newfound knowledge to progress to bigger and better things. It is certainly possible for the library to fulfill that promise. All the materials are there for any such persons who care to use them to broaden their personal horizons. But, in fact, those who make the greatest use of the institutions are not the disadvantaged or the poor. The typical library patron is middle class or, rather, upper middle class. The borrower has a managerial or professional position. It is apparent, then, that these library users are anything but the struggling poor.

The minority person—the black, the Puerto Rican, the chicano, the woman, the senior citizen—all these do not make as much use of the library. Here is an institution with limitless capacities for aiding the disadvantaged. All of us should learn what resources a library can offer and use them more fully, but especially those who have a longer way to go towards a fulfilling life than does the average mainstream American citizen. And the modern library has unique capacities for servicing just these people who need its free aid the most. A great outcry has gone up, in recent times, about the lack of cultural knowledge and information among nonwhites and ethnics. All over the country, universities have been opening up new departments for study of the culture and history of the heretofore neglected minorities: women's studies, Afro-American studies, Italian-American studies have become the order of the day. What institution has supplied the materials for these new areas of study?

In a corresponding development, libraries have begun to view themselves as cultural centers. They are making an effort to supply the needs of these groups. The library has recognized the fact, in some instances, that older types of foreign language books are inadequate to serve those Americans with different national origins. Librarians realize, for instance, that the Hispanic Americans are not a monolithic group. In some cases, they have attempted to provide cultural materials for the very distinct national origin groups of Spanish-speaking Americans such as Mexican-Americans, Cuban-Americans, and Puerto Ricans. The library can truly serve as a cultural center for all those who look to use it.

In some libraries, particularly in those in large cities, a very direct effort is being made to provide materials to Spanish-speaking peoples. An attempt is currently being made, in various sites throughout the country, to set up information centers especially for Latin Americans. Library personnel are not insensitive to the problems of the non-English speaker trying to make his or her way while using a foreign tongue.

Another interesting and, to me, vital service which new-style libraries are beginning to provide is that of a bureaucratic liaison and interpreter for citizens. Needless to say, government has become so complex and pervasive that the ordinary person barely knows where to begin when trying to deal with it. Libraries can, and many do, have special information centers designed to unravel the bureaucratic red tape. In the library, a person with a problem can learn which government agency would be most helpful. Help in filling out confusing forms can be obtained. True service to the community is provided in this way.

In this age of 40-odd percent unemployment among black teenagers, the young person needs all the help he or she can get. The good old corner library, again, may be the source of that help. All good libraries have vocational information. Moreover, many are developing outreach programs, itinerant, community libraries, to travel to the young person. Outreach programs for youth are a new and valuable focus for the institution, and one with great potential to involve the person who traditionally will never go near a staid and solemn library building.

Even as a source of entertainment, the library can be a great surprise and service. Many libraries have crafts shows. Records and audiovisual materials are available. In one New York City area library, filmmaking apparatus is lent out to community residents. Classes are offered in use of film equipment, and many valuable events are captured through these methods.

But to return to the stereotyped book distribution center—it was not such a bad idea, either. All of us can profit from the reading material every library has in great supply. Many of us can reach into our past and understand our present better through use of the library. The possibilities are limitless, if only we are willing to open its doors.

Elton C. Fax

DO WE BLACKS NEED PUBLIC LIBRARIES?

You bet we need them! We've always needed libraries and I'll tell you why I'm so convinced of it. You see, it all started with my knowing this small boy and his family a number of years ago. They were what folks commonly consider poor since they had barely enough money to cover their needs. Moreover, as a black family they were restricted to living in a segregated part of town. But that made little difference in how and what they felt about themselves. Never once did this family pretend to have what it didn't have, nor were the material things it lacked allowed to become the major issue in their lives.

> "You don't have to have money to be clean and decent, and you can certainly learn to *think* without having your pockets lined with money. Besides, people can steal your money, but once you fill your mind with knowledge *nobody* can steal that from you!"

It was a theme constantly heard around the house, a theme the children absorbed early and never forgot. Their mother forever harped upon the wisdom of learning. Before her marriage she had been a country schoolteacher and you know how it is with former teachers.

They never really quit teaching. The children's father had his own way of coming down hard in support of honesty and integrity, and the children remembered that too.

At Christmas the youngsters' gifts invariably included a few books. While the slim family budget limited the scope of the toys, the kids could always count on getting something to read. Standard fairy tales by the Brothers Grimm and by Hans Christian Andersen were great illustrated favorites, as were *Black Beauty* and *Treasure Island* which their mother read to the children. In the winter the boy I mentioned used to huddle close to the stove and gaze into the glowing coals as his mother read. There the goblins, pirates, assorted beasts, and lovely maidens illustrated in the books came alive for him as they danced and gyrated in the flames.

He liked the reading of poetry, too, especially that of Longfellow, Whittier, and Riley. But Paul Lawrence Dunbar was his favorite.

> "Dunbar is one of *our own* great men whose poems you must get to know."

With that brief introduction his mother would sail into a spirited reading of *In the Morning*, a poem in dialect about an exasperated mother trying to get her lazy son out of bed. Hearing his mother switch from normal speech to dialect was great fun for the listening youngster. But as soon as he was able to read fairly well his mother took him to the nearby branch of the public library to get a borrower's card.

> "Your father and I are too poor to buy you all of the books you should read, so you'll have to borrow from the public library. We're lucky it's free. Someday you'll be able to buy books for yourself. Still, you'll always need the library for certain things."

Elton C. Fax

By 1975 standards it wasn't much of a branch library. Its collection was small, its lighting poor, and its seats as comfortable as rocks. And, of course, there was the librarian. Through the child's vision she appeared formidable and forbidding. A pale, humorless, tight-lipped woman, her icy blue eyes saw everything he believed she shouldn't see. It would be several years before the child would have any contact with a black librarian. Still it was the only branch close enough to home for the boy to visit regularly. Black folks in his town didn't complain though. *Any* public library they could use was a blessing. Farther south the libraries refused to lend to them even though they paid taxes right along with white folks.

Every Saturday the youngster went to the library to return books he had taken out the previous week and to borrow new ones. His mother was strict about his returning what he borrowed, and returning them *on time!*

> "We have no money to pay out in overdue fines or for lost books. So you be careful. YOU HEAR ME?"

One steamy summer day the boy was idling through the house making the kinds of noises small boys make. His mother, busy at her sewing, looked up.

> "What on earth ails you, son? Why can't you settle down and be quiet in this weather? GOOD LORD!"

> "There's nuthin' to do—unless I go outside."

> "OUTSIDE? If you had sense enough to fill this thimble of mine you wouldn't want to rip and tear in the hot streets. Go get a book and read."

> "I read all my books. And it ain't Saturday. That's when I'm supposed to go to the library."

In the tradition of nonpermissive black parents she glared at him.

> "Don't you tell *me* what day it is, boy! And how many times have I told you about saying 'ain't'? Now you just take your bottom and march it straight to that library and bring something back here to read. And be quick about it, too! I'm going to time you. And don't you dare run in that hot sun if you don't want sunstroke. YOU HEAR ME?"

> "Yessum."

The youngster quickly and silently gathered his books as he contemplated the unreasonable inconsistency of adults. HURRY! TAKE YOUR TIME! It made no sense. What in the world was sunstroke anyway, and had his mother ever gotten it? Something told him this wouldn't be the time to ask her.

Besides, it didn't seem that hot to him at all.

Outside everything sizzled. Heat waves danced off the pavement, though the boy was barely conscious of them as he skipped merrily along. Several blocks from the house Fat Arthur's unattended ice cart dripped water on the street. Hm-m-m-m. Maybe there were some ice shavings inside. He loved to suck ice shavings and this looked like a windfall. He moved toward the cart. Oh-oh! There was nosey Mrs. Collins sweating and rocking along on bandy legs. Damn! He'd have to forego the ice shavings. That old woman had hawklike eyes and the biggest mouth in town. If he took one ice sliver she'd swear she'd seen him hijacking the whole cart! He'd better not ignore her either, or she'd tell *that*.

> "Good afternoon Miz Collins!"

> "Hello, sonny. How's your mother, Goin' to the li-berry?"

There she goes—prying as usual.

> "She's fine, Miz Collins. Yessum, I'm goin' to the li-berry."

He kept moving and had managed to scoot around the corner just as the old lady admonished him to be a good boy. The library, just opposite the firehouse, was in sight now. Hm-m-m-m! Wouldn't it be great if, at just this moment, the engines would be called out on a fire? But no such luck. Even the familiar dalmatian wasn't lazing at the entrance, having sensibly sought a cooler spot in some remote corner deep inside. The boy turned reluctantly away from the firehouse and slid into the library. He was relieved to find that the thin-lipped guardian of the desk was not on duty. Her place was temporarily filled by a younger woman who smiled sweetly as he surrendered his books over the desk.

> "Have you read any of the *Our Little Cousin* series? They are delightful and interestingly illustrated."

He hadn't and she led him happily to the stack.

> "Here they are. I'm sure you'll find something you'll like."

The youngster chose *Our Little Eskimo Cousin* and *Our Little Arabian Cousin.* When he got them home the illustrations caught his fancy and he began to read. He didn't stop until he had read both books. Then he read them over and over during the remainder of the week. And each time he went to the library thereafter he looked for other books in the series he hadn't seen before until he had read them all. Through those little books he gained his first glimpse of a vast and wondrous world and its peoples he had never before known.

These were no fairy tales about mythical beasts but descriptions of real humans with whom he could quickly form an identification. Although their appearance, customs, and languages differed from his own they reminded him of his own family. That was important to him. After all, the pattern of strict racial separation in his city permitted few meaningful interracial encounters. Indeed the pattern shrieked quite loudly that he and his people were unworthy of such encounters, though his parents assured him such was not the case. No barriers, however, kept him from feeling akin to his "little cousins" overseas with whom he visited through books from the library. Little did he then know what a significant thing had happened to him on that memorable summer's day visit to his branch library with the dim lights and the rocklike seats.

The boy grew up. He had studied, found a career, and his work had brought him not only satisfaction but an unexpected measure of world travel and public recognition. Reflecting upon his childhood he recalled that his learning through books began in his modest little home and from there spread to the public library. It was at home that he was taught that the acquisition of knowledge outranked the acquisition of material goods. Later, as a serious student, he learned that one never lives long enough or travels far enough to see and experience all that he needs and wants to know. Nor can one's mind accurately store, retain, and summon at will every fragment of information it has encountered. The really important thing, he found, was to know how and where to find such information as he needed. Most of it he sought and found in the public libraries.

He learned also that he was not alone in this—that other black Americans also knew how much our people need libraries. DuBois, Langston Hughes, Malcolm X, Gwendolyn Brooks, and Mary Bethune knew. And novelist Richard Wright certainly knew. Eager to read and prevented by custom from using the public libraries in his native Mississippi, Wright found a way. He cleverly deceived biased librarians into letting him take books they believed he was borrowing for white folks. And in Harlem, James Baldwin and historian John Henrick Clarke along with hundreds of others have made liberal and effective use of the Schomburg Collection of the New York Public Library.

So we (that small boy now grown—and I) enthusiastically share the love of libraries held by all those I have just mentioned and many more. Yes, that former boy and I often get together and "rap" about it all. To tell you the truth, we've never really ever been out of touch. You see, I was that kid.

Caroline Bird

ONE WOMAN'S USE OF LIBRARIES

I live and write in a rambling house on a pleasant lane in Dutchess County in upstate New York. It is beautiful in all seasons. There are birds, apple trees, and a view of the Hudson valley. My neighbors are charming, protective, and do not intrude when I am working. There is a good school for my son and space for his German shepherd.

My husband, who also writes, and I appreciate all this, but what really attracted us to the place is its proximity to three excellent libraries: the Adriance Memorial Library and the Vassar College Library in Poughkeepsie, and the Franklin D. Roosevelt Library in adjoining Hyde Park.

Since moving into this house in 1963, I have written five books largely from information obtained in or through these libraries. Three of these are in the feminist field as their titles indicate: *Born Female, Enterprising Women,* and *Everything a Woman Needs to Know to Get Paid What She Is Worth.*

At the same time, my husband has drawn on these libraries for three books and perhaps a hundred magazine articles. Some of the latter, about FDR's troubles in advancing the date of Thanksgiving and his stamp collecting, for example, have been written entirely from material in the Franklin D. Roosevelt Library.

As part of the National Archives, this library is public and open without charge to anybody interested in Franklin or Eleanor Roosevelt and their times. There you can study 38,000 books, 90,000 photographs, and 21 million pages of papers. You need only to have a project and some identification to obtain a pass good for a year. To serve scholars who spend their vacations researching, it is open on Saturdays in the summer. The adjoining museum is open every day except Christmas and is a great place to take children.

I have loved the cathedral-like Vassar College Library since I prowled its open stacks as a student. There are over 495,000 books and a new addition provides space for many more. While primarily for its students, the Vassar College Library serves others through interlibrary loans. Local teachers and ministers and certain other scholars living within 25 miles also may use it for a $10 annual fee which goes into the general college funds.

The Adriance Memorial Library, named for a public-spirited pioneer family, is the public library for Poughkeepsie. It dates from 1841 and is the oldest tax-supported library in the state. It has 128,000 books, also stereo records, motion picture films, and framed art reproductions you can borrow.

All three libraries are members of the Southeastern New York Library Resources Council, one of nine regional networks of largely academic and special libraries in the state. Council members borrow books that they do not own from each other, from the State Library at Albany, and sometimes from distant libraries. Southeastern even has a computer terminal connection with the Ohio College Library Center. Thanks to this I once borrowed a 100-year-old book from Oberlin College.

In addition to belonging to the Council, Adriance is the central reference library of Mid-Hudson Libraries, a five-county network of public libraries. This was organized in 1960 at the instigation of Mrs. Lettie Gay Carson, wife of Gerald Carson, the writer, to effect economies by mass purchasing and to provide better service. Sixty-two libraries are now members and it has served as a model for many other networks.

If I ask Adriance for a book not in its collection, it is sought in cards recording the holdings of other Mid-Hudson members. If one has it, I may have it the next day. If not the request may go to the Southeastern Council for a similar check or be teletyped to the State Library at Albany which has 4 million books and pamphlets and can usually comply. Requests for reference material are handled similarly. I sometimes receive photocopies of articles in old and rare journals from Albany in 48 hours. It is a state-financed service extremely valuable to writers.

But you do not have to be a writer to use your public library profitably. Whatever you want to be, or achieve, or acquire, the library is likely to be of help and usually without expense to you. The shelves are crowded with "how-to" books: "How to Sew," "How to Cook," "How to Lose Weight," "How to Dance," "How to Play Winning Tennis," "How to Amuse a Child," "How to Change Things," "How to Live a Rich Full Life—Cheap," and, of course, even "How to Write."

I have found a lot of excellent vocational guidance material in public libraries. There are books, bulletins, and government publications available describing the requirements, opportunities, rewards, and hazards of practically every kind of job, and, if it's a civil service spot, how to prepare for the examinations.

If you are applying for a job with a local company, a glance at what your library has about the company may give you exactly the information you need to impress an interviewer with your qualifications for it. If the company isn't right for you, this may save you a lot of grief.

If you want to keep informed about equal rights, the new opportunities for women, abortion, and other important women's issues of our time, look in your library. There are new books, magazines, newsletters, and abstract services devoted to these subjects. Every library has some of them. If enough women ask, they will obtain more.

If you have questions about your Social Security, income tax, or various benefits and are working, or even if you aren't, you may find it more convenient to consult your library in the evening than attempting to get into the government office involved during your lunch hour.

If you have to choose a college for yourself or a child, you will save yourself a lot of time, letter-writing, and a bit of postage by visiting the library that has a collection of the current catalogs on its shelves. Your postman also will be grateful.

If you need information on a company whose stock you own or are considering buying, you can find it in many public libraries in big fat volumes that are kept up-to-date with loose-leaf supplements that report the latest developments. Other volumes will give you the background of organizations that you may be asked to join or support.

If you can't remember the street address of Aunt Mildred in Minneapolis when you have to send her an important wedding invitation, your library may be able to supply it. Adriance and many others have shelves of out-of-town telephone and city directories and often are glad to look up an address or two in them while you hold the telephone.

They sometimes have other uses. My husband once wrote an article on the night riders of the American Revolution in which he recounted how William Dawes rode farther on the night of April 18, 1775, than Paul Revere (who contrary to Longfellow was captured by the British and robbed of his horse). As a consequence, George E. Dawes, a descendant of the horseman, wrote that he was forming an organization to honor his ancestor but that a firm compiling mailing lists from auto license records wanted to charge him $18,000 for a national list of people named Dawes. Tom suggested he look up Dawes in telephone directories in libraries.

Dawes and his relatives did so and formed the "Descendants of William Dawes Who Rode Association." It soon became a thriving organization with a newsletter and annual meetings. It held a rousing Bicentennial celebration of the famous ride in Boston in 1975. It has traced the Dawes genealogy back to 1620.

If you are interested in tracing your ancestors, it can be done more easily in libraries than in graveyards and parish records. *Searching for your Ancestors* by Gilbert H. Doane and many other books tell you how to do it. Some books are devoted to a single name. There are several periodicals devoted to the development of family trees.

I have found almost all librarians to be warm, friendly, competent people eager to help. I once needed a copy of the only known picture of Mary Goddard, the Baltimore woman who first printed the Declaration of Independence with the names of the signers. I obtained it simply by writing to the Enoch Pratt Free Library there (at a cost of $1.50, the photographer's fee). Nearly every library has an *American Library Directory* giving the names of librarians across the country to whom you can address requests of this sort.

If you can't come to the library, the library can often come to you. Adriance Memorial in Poughkeepsie, for example, has had for many years a service for temporary or permanent shut-ins. Adult and children's books, magazines, records, and pictures are available. The Brooklyn Public Library and many others have similar services for the disadvantaged. There are books in large type for those with impaired sight, and recordings and Braille publications for the blind.

Anybody in Vermont can obtain books by mail from the state's regional libraries. Printed catalogs listing and describing 1,650 of the volumes available are handed out in libraries and also mailed to users. They order the titles by mail or telephone. The special, low, library book rate for mailing material to and from libraries is the only postal rate that has not been increased sharply in recent years.

The Franklin D. Roosevelt Library is the oldest of the presidential libraries but new material is being added constantly and researchers frequently find something new in the old. One who did so not long ago was Dr. Nona Ferdon from the University of Hawaii working on a thesis.

She asked that the diary FDR started as a Harvard student be taken out of a glass display case so that she could read it. The archivists did so and she found that on four dates FDR's entries lapsed into a mysterious code of figures and truncated letters. When cryptographers failed to decipher these entries, she let the *Boston Globe* publish them.

Three readers promptly solved the code. Numbers had been substituted for vowels and some of the lines left off of other letters. The most interesting entry dated Groton, Connecticut, November 22, 1903, translated: "After lunch I have a never to be forgotten walk to the river with my darling."

Dr. Ferdon believes the "darling" was his future wife, Eleanor, and that he "could have confessed his love that day."

The last entry in the diary is definitely about Eleanor. Dated October 7, 1904, it says: "Still awful cold. Got E.R.'s ring at Tiffany's after much inspection and deliberation."

Lavinia Russ

SO NOW YOU ARE SIXTY?

It seemed that I was an absurd choice to be asked to write about what libraries have to offer those of us who find ourselves, in spite of ourselves, designated by that horrendous term, senior citizens. In the first place, I hadn't felt any different at sixty than I had at fifty. I feel no different now, at seventy, than I did at sixty. In the second place (and this seemed the ultimate of absurdities), I had never been in a library—not once in all my seventy years.

No, that's not quite true. I had scurried in and out of the children's rooms in libraries. (I earned my living selling, then writing, children's books, so I had to check what was displayed there.) But I *did* scurry in and out because a library to me was an institution, and I've always been terrified of institutions of any kind, and terrified of the people who worked in them. I always felt intimidated by my children's teachers. And to this day, I begin to break out in a sweat when I have to go to the bank. I rehearse silently (so far silently) as I walk to the bank, what I'm going to say. "I'd like the money like this," I rehearse, "two dollars in quarters, three dollars in dollars, ten dollars in fives, and two tens. Please?" Some reincarnation buff could probably explain my terror—convince me I had been a hermit, or perhaps a bank robber, in an earlier life—but the fact remains I'm chicken about any place that has a system.

I *did* once dare myself to walk between those two intimidating lions that guard the New York Public Library at Forty-second Street and Fifth Avenue to find a book in the adult section that I needed for an article I was writing. I was directed up to a room approximately as long as the Panama Canal. I gave one look at the endless rows of files, panicked, and rushed out to buy the book—an extravagance I could ill afford.

But perhaps I *wasn't* an absurd choice after all. For when I *did* discover at seventy the riches waiting for me at a library, I saw them all with the fresh wonder of the character who cried "Open Sesame!" and saw spread before his amazed eyes, the sparkling treasures revealed.

I also discovered all that I've missed in seventy years. I went to the Brooklyn Public Library, and even before I went through its wide doors, I began to discover how poor and narrow my life had been without a library in it. I had read a lot, yes. Books chosen for me by my parents when I was young, books I had chosen in bookstores from reviews when older, books recommended by friends. But here—inside those library doors—were not only books, but the universe itself. The words chiselled by the doors promised me that universe:

> Here are enshrined the longing of great hearts,
> And noble things that tower above the tide,
> The magic word that winged wonder starts,
> The garnered wisdom that has never died.

I had missed the joy that a young boy knew—a young boy who grew up to be Pete Hamill, the writer-columnist —the joy of finding helpful friends in the library who had helped him find the books he would enjoy, who were so helpful that he thought the words "great hearts" in the inscription referred to the librarians themselves.

I had missed the wealth of books on *any* subject, on *all* subjects—collections as vast and as varied as are the enthusiasms of the human heart. And I'd missed the librarians who cared, and who could and would find me the books I wanted—eager keepers of the flame.

But *that* discovery is obvious to anyone who has not been such a fool as I was for seventy years. Libraries have books for people who want to read books, and librarians to help people find the books they want.

But wait! Wait! Libraries have so much more besides books. Today they have, especially for those of us who have more time and leisure available, new worlds to discover. I wrote a book once about how to enjoy being a woman over sixty. I found the greatest hazards in growing older, besides the potentially obvious ones of reduced health and reduced incomes, were boredom and loneliness. I wish, oh how I wish, I had discovered a library before I completed the manuscript. For then I could have, would have, given a whole new chapter over to libraries because they are the conquerors of both boredom and loneliness.

There are, within the library walls, so many new countries of the mind and spirit to explore, as well as so many once-known countries to revisit, that if I listed them all, I should have no space left to write more than a hello and a goodbye. Before I describe some of the countries to tempt you to explore, let me list a few of the practical aids and suggestions that any respectable travel agent would bring to your attention.

If you, too, are new to libraries, it is a sound idea to get acquainted with your neighborhood library. The smaller staff there means a quicker meeting of minds for you and the librarian, who will know you by name, will know the kinds of books you like, the subjects you are interested in. And if the books are not on hand, the librarian will get them for you. He or she will have, or obtain for you in fast time, books in large print if your eyesight is no longer as strong as your interests. (If you are wise, you will also plan your visits to a library to get your books in the morning or early in the afternoon before the student rush fills the chairs, and absorbs the librarians' attentions.)

If you have a friend or a member of your family who is blind, the librarian will have, or be able to obtain from a larger library, cassettes or records—of great or entertaining classics or current books, read by fine actors, actresses, and other excellent readers.

If you or a friend is unable, through illness, to come to a library, you can order books by mail—through what is called Homebound Service. All you need is to get an envelope from the library—and the signature of your attending physician. Check your reading interests on the list enclosed within the envelope: *fiction* (romance, adventure, mystery, science fiction, etc.); *non-fiction* (science, history, art, government, etc.); *biographies* (current figures / nineteenth century / eighteenth century / earlier); *books written in foreign languages* (specify which); *hobbies* (bird watching, flowers, minerals, stamps, etc.).

In a larger, central type of library, you'll be wise if you stop at the desk by the door, for the young man or woman sitting there is especially trained to tell you the quickest route to the book you want. Also available there will be information about the newest, as well as future, exhibits and events that are taking place within the library.

And what splendid exhibits and events they are! If I described all that I was shown or told about in one afternoon at the Brooklyn Public Library, I would, as I said earlier, have no room left to list them. But here are a few, for those of us who are wise enough to use our leisure time to increase our knowledge of an established hobby, to explore the pleasures of a new hobby, to enrich our hearts with music and pictures, to widen our vision with new points of view about old and new experiences and events.

There are clubs to join—stamp clubs or chess clubs, to mention only two. (No, I can't resist a third—there is a *magic* club!)

There are movies to see. (I had a hard time deciding, from a myriad of titles, between the thirteen-part color film series, *Civilisation*, narrated by Sir Kenneth Clark; and *Auntie Mame.*)

There are exhibits of pictures—with the artists themselves often at hand. There are music recitals to enjoy. There are exhibits that highlight different countries—a week of a cultural festival. (Scandinavia and India were two of the countries or regions that the Brooklyn library had recently highlighted). In our multicultural world, there will be many more festivals, among which may well be a celebration of your own ancestral land. (An aside—there are books printed in forty languages at the Brooklyn library, as well as classes for those of us who would like to improve our reading skills in a particular language.)

There are exhibits, classes, and discussion groups to appeal to any hobby, any interest you can name: from photography to flowers, from Afro-American history to women's consciousness-raising, from transcendental meditation to travel tips, from tales of Israel to tales of your own neighborhood.

And those are just a sampling! Besides these, there the paperbacks to borrow; newspapers, local and foreign; and magazines to read in comfort and in company, when we grow tired of being alone.

All this, and a haven, too, are here for you in a library. The whole wide world is yours when you cross the threshold of your library doors.

Norman Cousins

AN IMPORTANT PORT OF CALL

Libraries have long been stores of inspiration for imaginative travelers. Their books do more than provide them with an itinerary of places to see—they make those places come alive. But many travelers fail to recognize that using a library *during* a trip is even more important than using it in advance of a trip. Wandering through the aisles in a foreign library can give an American a vital sense of the political, cultural, and social topography of that country—and of his own country as well.

When I visited the Lenin Library in Moscow, for example, I asked the librarian about the American novels most in demand. It turned out that Mitchell Wilson's books—which never received much attention in the United States—had the highest popularity. The answer was as revealing as it was unexpected; Wilson's books deal with the conflicts experienced by scientists—conflicts between their social obligations and their work on atomic weaponry.

The Lenin Library's section on sanitary engineering was immense, and crowded with browsers. The same was true in New Delhi, where agriculture texts were also popular. People in those countries are hungry for technical knowledge. My library visits were probably more reliable sources for that conclusion than any statistical studies.

One afternoon during the Korean War, I paid a visit to the United States Information Service (USIS) library in Taegu. I watched for hours as the South Koreans moved freely about the open book and magazine stacks. Some were refugees fresh from the war zone, now spreading fast toward Taegu. Some were youngsters of high school age. Many appeared to be middle-aged or older. Doubtless, some came in to stay out of the cold, hardly a crime in itself.

Toward the front of the one large room was a magazine rack. Seldom have I seen the printed word or picture put to greater use. Some of the periodicals were a year or more old. They had been patched and repatched until they were hardly recognizable. But the young folks, bundled in their bulky rags, would go through them hungrily. The world that turned in front of them and that passed through their fingers was a world tinged with magic, for it told of a land free of war where people lived in their own homes and tilled their own soil and sent their children to heated schools. I can't read faces well enough to tell, but I had the feeling that the emotion these young folks knew was not envy so much as wonder and perhaps even hope that these were the things that Americans wanted not only for themselves but for their fellow human beings.

The story was much the same elsewhere. In Calcutta I found the American library after walking through involved alley entrances, climbing stairs, and solving the puzzle of intricate corridors. But these natural hazards did not keep the Calcutta library from being one of the busiest places in the city. In Cairo I met agricultural students who acknowledged their great debt to American agricultural research, as reported in books and professional journals available at the local American library. However small these libraries were, however crowded or hard to find, they were accomplishing an important undertaking: they were showcases of American freedoms, of which the freedom to read and think is the most important.

That the showcase is genuine is something that became vividly apparent to me several years ago. I was pitted against a Soviet in a radio debate being broadcast in India. My opponent seemed bent on establishing two facts. First, that Howard Fast was the greatest American novelist. Second, that the vaunted American freedom of the press was a joke because Fast was banned in the United States. Fast had won the Stalin International Peace Prize, so I wasn't surprised that my colleague had singled him out. But I knew that the author's writings had significance for other countries, too. Fast had explored man's various struggles for freedom, and used that theme in fictionalized accounts of the Roman slave revolt, the American revolution, the labor movement, and even Israel's ancient fight for freedom. Without disparaging Fast, I suggested that there were many American literary critics who might differ on the name of the "best" American writer. In any event, our Indian listeners were in the happy position of being able to read Fast's books in the USIS library and make their own evaluation. As for the charge of "banning," its absurdity became apparent in the very fact that Fast's writings were between book covers in an American library just around the corner. I knew they were there; I had seen them myself.

Visiting those libraries did much to show me the impact of American thought on other cultures. But creativity, in the end, is first and foremost a human product, not a national one. The best of libraries finds a niche for its own authors in a spectrum of worldwide literary output.

Libraries in Japan have accomplished this task with exquisitely comprehensive collections. When Japanese readers discuss current literary trends, their yardstick is far from being a purely national one. Their evaluations are far-reaching; they like to refer to writers from France or the United States whose work invites comparison with their own authors. And when they meet with foreign visitors, their relish in relating their work to the outside world is clearly evident.

When I visited the library in Tokyo, I asked some scholars there to name the books, regardless of language, that have had the greatest impact on Japanese thought and writing. They agreed to exclude the great religious books as being too obvious. Thus, Confucius, whose literary significance in the East was exceeded only by his religious influence, was declared ineligible. Finally, they came up with ten titles of books they thought the Japanese would consider the greatest books ever written:

1. Collected works of Shakespeare
2. Dante's *Divine Comedy*

3. Poems of Tu-Fu (China, circa 720 A.D.)
4. Goethe's *Faust*
5. Tolstoi's *War and Peace*
6. Works of Plato
7. Works of Aristotle
8. Lady Murasaki's *Tales of Genji*
9. Cervantes's *Don Quixote*
10. Works of Stendhal.

What I marvelled at, in this list, was its overall balance and grasp of world writing. Equally significant, perhaps, was the fact that it would be difficult today to hold a general discussion with American or European literary critics who would have equal familiarity with Asian literature. It is not only our students who are ill-prepared for the world of ideas today; our teachers, philosophers, and writers as a group unhappily suffer from a time lag of a century or more in their awareness of Eastern culture.

In a more general sense, we are all victims of disconnection and acceleration. We don't have time to familiarize ourselves with every thought, every idea, every book everywhere on earth. The modern world has confused us and threatened us as well. Man has been projected as from the mouth of a cannon onto a world stage with no rehearsal in the part of the world citizen he is called upon to play. Moreover, he is bewildered by the multiplicity of players with their strange accents and even stranger actions. There is much he doesn't like about it and a great deal he fears. All he knows is that he is involved beyond exemption or recall.

But whatever the uncertainties about the future may be, of one fact we can be sure. The present generation and the next generation and the generations after that will have to be citizens of the human community. They will have to be at home in many lands and among many peoples. They will have to talk many languages and comprehend many philosophies, psychologies, and approaches that are now uncharted in much of present-day American education. Finally, they will have to know how to look for and appraise information about the world of ideas and events. Their country is going to have to make the biggest decisions in its history—both for the purpose of assuring its own survival and for helping to keep this planet in a single piece—and this will require some inspired prodding by the individual citizen.

The library has the means to nourish and, indeed, to inspire. Wherever it may be located, the library is not just another shrine to visit. A library, to modify the famous metaphor of Socrates, is the delivery room for the birth of ideas—a place where history comes to life.

The book is no substitute for travel; neither is travel a substitute for the book. Going to foreign places is an adventure, but more exciting still is seeing that spark of fraternity when one man comes to understand the ideas —or the ideals—of another. For that reason, the library is important to anyone who travels in the world. And it is essential for those who want to live in it.

Josette Frank

LIBRARIES ARE A PARENT'S BEST FRIEND

"When the children drive me to distraction at home, I take them to the library. It's my last resort!" This remark from a young suburban mother surprised me—I have always thought of the library as a *first* resort. This mother probably will, too, when she discovers that the library is a parent's best friend.

Perhaps she should have begun earlier to recognize the persuasive power of books and the listening power of children, not to mention the enchantment of pictures. As a young child begins to understand words and recognize pictures, parent and child together can share the pleasure of books. The very fact of this sharing gives to books a special aura; the child discovers early that books are a source of delight. This doesn't call for loading the home shelves with a large assortment of books. A very few well-selected picture books at home, hard-paged or even paperbacks, and a good picture Mother Goose, are enough for the very young listener who wants to hear them over and over again.

But as children outgrow their baby books, no home can provide the wealth of books to explore that the public library can. "Explore" is the key word here, for parent and child alike. If you have ever watched a four-year-old literally tear into the picture-book shelves in the children's section of the library you have realized that a whole world is opening up to him.

The problem then becomes: how to choose from this bountiful supply? Certainly all these books must be "good"—they have been carefully selected by knowledgeable librarians. But even very young children have their special interests and preferences. Not every "good" book has sure-fire appeal for every child. Some may want stories about animals, other prefer the pictured workings of machines and trucks, or stories about children doing familiar things; some like funny stories ("real silly"), some don't. Books of all these kinds are there for the finding. Parents who have watched their children's preferences at home will seek out a librarian who can guide them to a book or books which match these interests, or perhaps expand them.

Should you turn the children loose to choose their own? The preschooler is all too likely to be attracted by a cover or a picture in a book you are sure he will not enjoy. No matter; it's a triumphant act of choice! Most libraries are generous in allowing you to take home several books, so you can quietly take along another one or two you think more likely to appeal. At home read first the child's own chosen book, and your choices next. You may even have some surprises! And these will guide you in your next selections. The book he wants read over and over again (no matter that *you* are weary of it) you had better renew when it's due at the library—or buy a copy for him to keep for his very own.

While you may have to keep an eye on your preschooler's handling of library books, too much admonishing to "handle with care" may turn off their pleasure in books. A little intervention can go a long way. And your own careful handling of books is likely to carry this message.

Then there are the weekly story hours at the library. However much we enjoy reading with our children, telling stories calls for quite another skill, and not all parents have it. The library's trained storyteller holds the children spellbound, and may well suggest new interests to pursue. The presence and responses of other children involve them all in the story. It's fun at the library!

As children grow older and books more familiar, boys and girls are likely to know exactly what they are looking for, and quickly find their way to the shelves of their choice. Whether they want factual science books or horse stories, adventure or mystery, or another in their current, endless "series books," they choose their book with a quick eye, and clutch it tightly. It's usually impossible to deflect them or to substitute something you consider more "worthwhile." Nor is it wise. But again you may want to browse among your own remembered favorites or ask the children's librarian to suggest one or two titles, and quietly take them along home. Leave them where the children can find them; but don't push! Offer to read them to the children if their reading skills haven't yet reached that far. They may turn down your offer, but they'll remember those titles when they meet them on the library shelves next year. Curiosity may do the rest.

But it may also be that some of the books remembered from your childhood are dated for today's young readers. And don't forget, too, that many very good books have been published since your childhood reading years. You may well enjoy reading some of these yourself, guided by current reviews in magazines and newspapers, or suggested in the selected lists prepared by librarians and other children's book specialists. Not the fiction only, but some of the superb nonfiction being published today for young readers—books on science subjects especially—might prove equally informative to adults who want to know "just enough" about such awesome matters as atomic energy, or how to change over to the metric system. Often these so-called "juveniles" succeed in making complicated concepts clear, readable, and understandable for those of us who need to keep up with our children in this fact-filled world.

By the time they become teenagers, girls and boys are off on their own and the library becomes their private preserve. Confirmed readers may read anything and everything, from newspapers and comics to racy magazines, from so-called classics to current best sellers you may not approve. Some, of course, will still specialize in books that serve their long-time interests. Others may concentrate on books from the required school reading lists, selecting from among these the easiest, or the shortest, or the best, according to their bent.

Maybe now they don't need or want your guidance in their reading choices any more; maybe you've given up on what you consider their "far out" reading; but you still have a role: what *you* read may, in itself, suggest what you consider "good." And if they value their parents' opinions—and, surprisingly, many young people do—they may pass along some of their own new-found literature for you to read. Even if they don't accept your judgment of their preferred reading, a give-and-take discussion may clear the reading air between the generations.

I remember, some years ago, a fourteen-year-old to whom a classmate had smuggled a copy of J. D. Salinger's *Catcher in the Rye.* At that time this was surreptitious reading. This boy had the bright idea of bringing it home and suggesting that his father read it. Needless to say, his father, not very understanding of adolescent boys, was startled—but found he had learned from this reading a great deal about his son's emotional maturing. I gather this was the educational result his son had had in mind!

Incidentally, for fathers as well as mothers, the library is a source that can be tapped for helpful books about child development and the art and skill of parenting. There is so much knowledge about childhood that doesn't necessarily come to us out of our own parental experiences. Books can sometimes open the way to fresh insights. There are thoughtfully selected lists to help in the wise choice of such books. Some libraries also offer programs of lectures or discussion groups on subjects of particular interest to parents, especially about children's reading and book selection.

It's good to know that libraries are increasingly aware of the varied needs of the communities they serve. Some neighborhood libraries collect and keep on file useful information about many services that are available in their community: day-care centers, clinics, welfare agencies, civic groups, and other resources.

And one more word: When you take your children to the library to select their books, if you take home some books from the adult shelves for your own reading, you suggest to them that libraries are for adults too—a good thing for them to learn early!

Dorothy Rodgers

IT'S ALL YOURS—AND IT'S FREE!

I am a curious person—not peculiar or even mildly eccentric, just interested in almost everything. And, for someone like me, there can never be enough time to read as much as I would like. Clearly, I can't hope to own all the books I want to read and, happily, I don't have to worry about that. Our public libraries are so accessible that I can take advantage of them at my convenience.

Since a large part of my life has been concerned with the pleasure—and pain—of running a household, I've chosen to focus on the ways in which a library can be particularly useful to a housewife.

It's natural for me to start by writing about cookbooks because I've had a lifelong interest in food and its preparation. I am incapable of ignoring a printed recipe. No matter how hard-pressed I may be for time, books about food have an irresistible claim on my attention. The world may be falling apart, but I can always manage to make time to look through a cookbook. I will, at least, glance at the name of the dish; if it stars marshmallows, peanut butter, and maraschino cherries, I can and do, with no effort at all, resist reading further. But if, as is more likely, the recipe presents instructions for a variation on an old favorite or a new and intriguing combination, I not only read it with care, I savor each ingredient and make a decision either to copy the recipe for future use—or to reject it.

But with the masses of cookbooks being published in a seemingly endless stream—from paperbacks on cooking for one-armed diabetic computer operators, to encyclopedic, handsomely illustrated, and wildly expensive volumes, the problem of satisfying my desire to explore them all becomes more and more difficult. Without access to a public library, it's virtually hopeless. Most women own one or two standby cookbooks on which they depend—and that serve them well; but many of us who like to cook enough to want to experiment, can't afford to buy all the books we would enjoy looking through. I am fascinated by the foods of different countries—and by the differences in style within countries; northern cookery versus southern, hearty peasant fare as opposed to formal dishes, painstakingly prepared. I often find myself choosing only one or two recipes from a book of hundreds. Probably I am not alone in being so selective, but this kind of luxury can only be indulged because there are public libraries. There I am free to browse, to copy what appeals to me—or to take some of the books home to read at my leisure.

Although food is certainly one of the important aspects of homemaking, there are many other areas that could be more imaginatively managed with help by the intelligent use of a library. When my husband and I decided, about ten years ago, to build a house, I went over the notes I had been storing for many years—notes for a dream house that I didn't ever expect to have the chance to build. I knew what we had liked about the houses we had lived in and, even more important, I knew what we hadn't liked. This was all to the good, but I wanted to look at photographs of houses, interiors, and gardens, and I wanted to learn about new materials, appliances, and fixtures with which I wasn't familiar. This could only be done by going to the public library and putting myself in the knowledgeable hands of a kind librarian who would help me find my way around. It was enormously helpful to let my eyes wander over the hundreds of photographs in dozens of books—here approving, there adapting—or disliking—all kinds of details.

Whether you're building a house, remodeling, designing a room, or merely recovering a piece of furniture, your imagination is stimulated by seeing what professionals have done with similar problems. You can learn to avoid the obvious pitfalls, become aware of how skillful use of color can emphasize a room's good points, camouflage its weaknesses, or create an illusion of added dimension. You can recognize the difficulties involved in blending patterns or periods and the importance of scale. Finally, you can discover which areas are too complicated for the amateur; paying for expert advice can often save money in the long run—and prevent the disappointments that come from inexperience.

No matter how much experience we've had in entertaining our friends, most of us welcome new ideas and approaches. Books on that subject are almost as numerous as cookbooks! Are you planning a wedding reception—or a Halloween party for children? A game party for teenagers or a brunch, a cocktail party or a buffet dinner for your own friends? Compare different menus suggested and ways of serving and choose the style that suits you best. For hobbyists, "how-to" books abound. Do you want to know the ins and outs of collecting anything and everything? Perhaps it's flower arrangements you're interested in, or maybe you'd like to know which plants can be best cultivated indoors. Would you like to learn about the art of furniture finishing or how to make minor repairs about the house? Take advantage of those who've done it—and written about it. Go to the library and read up on it!

My own hobbies, besides cooking, include sewing and needlepoint. In the last few years books about needlepoint have been produced with bewildering rapidity. They cover the field—from books for neophytes to books for ultrasophisticates. By seeing what is available on all these subjects, you may well decide there are some books that are so indispensable that you want to own them. Put their titles on a list and treat yourself to one from time to time. Besides your own list, you may want to ask for pamphlets prepared each year by many libraries giving suggestions for books in various classifications. The books have been reviewed and chosen with great care and the pamphlet could prove especially useful in choosing books to buy for children.

Children's books are so much more imaginative and interesting than they were during my own childhood, but their cost has skyrocketed in the past few years and only through libraries can children have access to the whole range published today. There can be no better way to instill—and insure—a lifelong habit of reading than to expose a child to the diverse pleasures libraries have to offer.

Besides books, there are all kinds of attractions to appeal to a variety of children's interests: storytelling hours for small children where the readers are so skillful that they read upside-down so that the children can follow the illustrations, (actually I've learned their trick—they memorize the stories!); arts and crafts sessions, tongue-twisting contests, magic shows, puppet shows, and plays in which the children take an active part—helping to make the scenery, props, and costumes. Films are often shown and there are listening rooms for music. How lovely that the records, cassettes, films—and, of course, books—can be taken home for hours of enjoyment.

Parents can share these joys with their children—and there's help for them, too. Librarians tell tales of parents with glazed eyes who wander into the libraries the day after Christmas asking pathetically for books that can teach them how to look after hamsters, gerbils, snakes, or other livestock that have been given to the children.

Not the least of library service is the dedication and helpfulness of the people who work in them. Librarians, as a breed, are friendly, helpful, informed—and often witty. They love what they're doing and most of them will take no end of trouble to help you find what you're looking for. Libraries offer such a feast that it would be ridiculous for me to do more than try to remind you of what you already know: they are the keepers of knowledge; they cherish our civilization; and they hold the keys to the future. Best of all, they're all yours—and they're free!

R. A. Clem Labine

CAN THIS HOUSE BE SAVED?

We had just taken title to our 1884 Victorian brownstone. My wife, looking blithely past the damage the structure had suffered in its forty years as a rooming house, was grandly envisioning entertaining friends at high tea in the formal parlor before Christmas. Surely, she reasoned, five months was ample time to restore an old house! Since neither of us had ever wielded anything more complicated than a paint brush, I was in no position to dispute her.

Eight years later (having missed the original goal by several Christmases), we are far wiser and a bit more skilled in some of the arcane crafts of house restoration—and we shudder at the naive innocence with which we initially approached our brown elephant. More than once it took some quick research at our library to get us out of a bind that our brashness had gotten us into. Like the time that I had assured my wife that I could restore some plaster cove molding that some long-ago overflowing bathtub had destroyed. Of course I had no idea *how* I was going to bring this miracle about, since my experience with plaster had been limited to patching cracks in walls with a can of premixed spackle. Finally, in the library, I discovered a manual that was designed for teaching apprentices who were learning the plasterer's trade. And in those pages—thank heaven—all the mysteries of ornamental plaster were revealed.

Our experience is being duplicated by owners of homes—old and new—all over the country. For a house is a living organism, just as surely as is a tree or a mushroom. A house is constantly in motion; it expands and contracts, material is added or taken away, it grows and decays. Maintaining a house is doing battle continuously with the basic forces of nature that are trying to return the structure to the dust of the earth.

There was a time when most homeowners could hire a little help in this battle with the elements. But sheer economic necessity is forcing the householder to be more self-reliant. The neighborhood handyman, who could be hired at reasonable rates and would do reliable work, has gone the way of the Huppmobile. Even such other worthies as the local plumber and contractor are getting more expensive and scarce. Any day now I expect my plumber to announce that he is no longer making house calls.

How then is the homeowner supposed to acquire the skills to improve his or her home—or merely to keep it from crumbling into dust? Among the crafts and skills that the householder can profitably employ in the maintenance and repair of the home are: roofing, masonry, plumbing, electrical wiring, wood refinishing, plastering, paperhanging, carpentry, painting and decorating, and interior design. Unless you can afford to spend two years as an apprentice to a master craftsman, the only other way to learn these skills is—BOOKS.

But getting to the *right* books definitely is not simple. And that's where libraries provide a stable and sane element of continuity in this tumultuous world. Book publishers in recent years have been pouring out new titles at a dizzying rate. As a result, newspapers and magazines can review only a small fraction of them. And bookstores will only stock the fastest moving titles. So books of highly specialized interest—like *How to Build and Repair Fireplaces*—are not likely to get prominent display anywhere. Yet these specialized problem-solving volumes are just what the homeowner needs.

The library rescues the neophyte handyperson by performing for books the same function as a tool catalog serves for handtools: an incomparable showcase. In a good tool catalog you get a chance to see more tools displayed than even the largest hardware stores can exhibit. As a result, you have a better chance of finding the tool that's just right for your particular problem. Similarly, a library gives you a chance to sample the widest range of books on any given topic—whether you use the card catalog in an orderly fashion or just scan the shelves.

There are some books—such as a basic home-repair manual—that you'll want to purchase for your own bookshelf. The library allows you to browse through all that are available so that you can select the one that's right for you—before laying out the ten to fifteen dollars that such books go for these days.

And of course there will be those other books that you'll use only once—perhaps a treatise on the repair of stained glass—and here the library's traditional function of lending such volumes can save many dollars in purchase costs.

Because of the Bicentennial and the growing interest in preservation, there has been increasing interest among homebuyers in the purchase and restoration of vintage houses—generally defined as those built prior to 1914. These present some special difficulties for the owners because most of the information in the standard do-it-yourself magazines and manuals is aimed at houses built after 1920. But in vintage houses, the owner is very likely to find many oddities (by today's construction standards) in such things as: foundation construction, masonry materials, framing system, partition construction, roofing materials, mechanical systems, and decorative detailing. If the owner is intent upon restoring the house to its original glory, the first challenge may be to discover just how its original glory looked. Many old houses have been "remuddled" totally out of character by thoughtless prior owners.

The library is indispensable to the old-house buff. First, the library is likely to have dusty old volumes of local history—photos that will show, if not your house, then ones very close to it and how they looked when new. Too, the library is the best place to start accumulating information about the specialized publications that deal with old architecture, such as *History News, Preservation News, The Bulletin of the Association for Preservation Technology*, and *The Old-House Journal.*

When the challenge is to duplicate some old ornamental plasterwork, or to re-create some decorative woodwork that has disappeared over the years, the library may well be the *only* source that will be able to produce the book you need. The library will also be invaluable in turning up books that deal with authentic period decorating schemes for the finished house. Don't expect to find this kind of help in the monthly "shelter" publications.

For example, one of the most valuable sources for decorating ideas for our Victorian brownstone was: *Decorative Art of Victoria's Era* by Frances Lichten. This book, available through our public library, is now quite rare, and try though I might I have not been able to locate a copy that I might purchase.

It's in the preservation of out-of-print books that libraries perform perhaps their most important function. Book publishers today are regarding books more and more like boxes of breakfast cereal: something to be loaded onto the shelves this month, only to be moved out next month when a newer, hotter product comes along. As a result, many valuable books appear in bookstores for a few months, spend a few more months on the remainder tables, and then, like a spent meteorite, disappear from commerce forever. Their useful lives are extended only by the shelter afforded them on library shelves. Important works on period decoration like Larry Freeman's *New Light on Old Lamps* and H. L. Peterson's *Americans at Home* are now available only through libraries.

Whether you are doing work yourself, or are merely supervising someone else to make sure the job is done right, today's homeowner needs to have at least a passing acquaintance with a dozen crafts. The library is your "union card"—your passport to this world of specialized skills.

Vartanig G. Vartan

INFORMATION FOR INVESTORS

When I first came to New York City as a financial news reporter—fresh from covering politics, court trials, whisky still raids and other sports events in Mississippi—I decided the best place to start learning about the world of business and Wall Street was the public library. So I marched up to the desk of the main reading room on Forty-second Street, presented my book slips, received a number, and then sat down to await the volumes that would impart knowledge. But my number never appeared on the announcing board. Only later, after I had left in dismay, did I learn that there were two sides to the room; I had an odd number and was seated, blissfully ignorant of all instruction signs, in the even number section. Since that time my success in using libraries for research purposes has improved considerably.

Similarly, I came to find that for investors the shelves of a library can turn into rich lodes for mining. I applied the walk-before-you-run (or the survey-before-you-pickaxe) thesis and can recommend it to others. First, there is the opportunity to form a general frame of reference by reading books. This involves acquiring a historical perspective on investing, a basic knowledge of how markets work, and a discovery of the various opportunities open to the public.

The next step in background reading can involve more specialized books concerning various phases of investing. Within the last several years, for example, gold and other precious metals have taken on special luster during a period of high inflation. Real estate and commodities have benefitted from the same factors. Even within the field of securities, stocks do not necessarily rule supreme. Thus, it behooves the investor to acquire a working knowledge of fixed-income instruments, such as corporate bonds, treasury bills, tax-exempt municipal bonds, and preferred stocks. At the same time, one should acquire a basic familiarity with such diverse areas as mutual funds, the over-the-counter market, stock charts, buying on margin, and growth stocks.

Some people, of course, bring with them varying degrees of sophistication about investing. They may wish to skip the preliminaries and get on with acquiring more specialized information. But, regardless of the background a person carries into the library, a good part of the enjoyment exists in individual exploration. As one learns more about the varied spheres of investing, he may naturally develop a taste or interest for certain areas. Thus, older investors whose prime aim may be the preservation of capital might naturally seek to know more about bonds than speculative stocks.

Vartanig G. Vartan

There are a number of good basic books about securities investing. I might suggest two of them—*The Intelligent Investor* by Benjamin Graham (New York: Harper, 1973), and *The Battle for Investment Survival* by G. M. Loeb (New York: Simon & Schuster, 1965). Similarly, *Financial Handbook* by J. I. Bogen (New York: Ronald, 1968) can serve as a richly detailed primer.

The main purpose served by this reading, be it fundamental or at a more specialized level, is to create a basis for judgments on the part of the individual. As such, it provides vital background about the investment process and supplies a person with the necessary equipment for probing and asking questions. When your dentist recommends the removal of an impacted tooth, chances are that you'll go along with his suggestion. But in dealing with brokers (security, commodity, or real estate) it is good basic procedure to ask a lot of questions and then to test the answers against the frame of reference you can acquire in a library.

The second part of the walk-before-you-run thesis deals with the more topical and current material which often is to be found in periodical rather than book form. Once an investor has built up his sense of awareness, he naturally may be in the market for more contemporary information. The two best newspapers for this source material are the *New York Times* and the *Wall Street Journal*. Other publications that can prove of value include *Barron's*, *Forbes*, *Value Line Investment Survey*, *Wall Street Transcript*, Moody's *Stock Survey*, Standard & Poor's *Outlook*, and *Commercial & Financial Chronicle*.

These publications, as well as such advisory services as Babson's, T. J. Holt, and Anametrics, contain current data on industries as well as individual companies. Often they suggest specific investment advice (which may or may not prove valid—that's a key reason for creating a basis for judgments).

One advantage of reading current periodicals and newspapers is that they often contain investment developments and opportunities that, because of a time lag, have yet to appear in book form. For example, during the period of record-high interest rates in 1974, the most popular form of mutual fund was a newcomer known as the money-market fund. These funds invest in commercial paper, bank certificates of deposit, and government securities that typically are shut off to many smaller investors. The appeal of the money-market funds became the high rate of return (and instant redeemability) that they offered. Similarly, options trading has become a popular form of speculation within the last year or two for more venturesome investors who want to commit only a relatively small and finite portion of their capital in hopes of achieving capital gains.

Meanwhile, two basic reference works that contain current data on companies (in a factual sense, rather than offering investment suggestions) are the various manuals published by Moody's and by Standard & Poor's.

A corollary wealth of information is contained in libraries for businessmen and businesswomen who may wish to sharpen their decision-making processes, learn more about their prospective fields as a means of job advancement, or perhaps even investigate opportunities in some new area. Indeed, one of the more striking developments in the last few years has been the desire of many men and women to switch careers, either because of boredom, or lack of opportunity for growth, or necessity growing out of a family situation.

Many libraries offer books in subject areas ranging from economics, banking, and management to advertising, taxation, personnel, and business law. Similarly, current publications run the gamut from *Business Week* and the *Harvard Business Review* to works produced by the Department of Commerce and the Bureau of the Census.

One effective way to draw attention to libraries—and thereby attract greater participation by investors and persons in the business community—is to hold seminars or evening talks. Thus, a stockbroker or a tax expert or a local businessman can help to educate other people through the physical facilities of the library. Another method is to show films on the various aspects of investing; the New York Stock Exchange, for example, offers a program to provide such films free of charge.

[A final word of advice for investors in the New York City area (who presumably already know how to secure books in the Main Reading Room of the public library): the firm of Merrill Lynch, Pierce, Fenner & Smith, Inc. has a splendid reference library which is open to the public at One Liberty Plaza, located only a few blocks from the Stock Exchange. This library contains a rich lode of corporate files, including annual reports, prospectuses, and proxy statements for individual companies. Also, the Business Library of the Brooklyn Public Library is an exemplary institution which may be utilized both by investors and the business community.]

Roger Ebert

LIBRARY LIFE OF A FILM CRITIC

One thing a movie critic is always being asked is how many times a week he goes to the movies. Four or five times, I say, not counting the movie class I teach and the classics I may go to see again, and the late show on television. And during film festivals, of course, the total may reach three or four movies a day.

This consumption of film immediately makes me seem, to the layperson, an object of curiosity, and I'm often asked if I went to the movies a lot as a kid. I sure did, I say; I spent every Saturday afternoon at the Princess Theater on Main Street in Urbana, Illinois, absorbed in the doings of the Bowery Boys, Hopalong Cassidy, and even young Mr. Lincoln. And then in high school and college I went to movies whenever I got the chance.

That's my story, and it's more or less true, but when a reporter from my hometown paper asked my mother not long ago if I really went to the movies all the time, she said that wasn't the way she remembered it: during one summer, she recalled, I read sixty-four books at the Urbana Free Library and won the reading contest. I'd forgotten that laurel, but she was correct; and during the next summer I undoubtedly read more, because I read my way around the children's room and made great inroads on the adult stacks, and was undoubtedly much more literate in literature than in film on the day I wrote my first movie review.

The librarian I remember best is Mrs. Bernice Fiske, who not only masterminded the library's marionette shows every Saturday, but also seemed to have a special gift for suggesting a new author just when her young readers were ready for one. I went from the Dr. Dolittle series to the books about the Melody Family by Elizabeth Enright (each one read at least a dozen times), and then to Mary O'Hara and Booth Tarkington. I didn't just read *Penrod*; I studied it, and envied Penrod for being the Compleat Boy with a proper base of operations (disused horse stable, an extensive alley system) and the correct tools (penknife, flintstone).

Urbana was also the location, of course, of the great University of Illinois Library, and when I was a little older I'd ride my bike over to the campus and walk, solemnly and (I hoped) invisibly, through the vast main reading room with its Penn Station ceiling. An original copy of Audubon's *Birds of North America* was kept under glass and a page was turned every day: I regarded it with awe, as I did Vol. 1, No. 1 of *Life* magazine (when a friend of the family checked it out of the stacks for me).

I've always been a voracious reader, one with an instinctive sympathy for Thomas Wolfe's Eugene Gant, roaming hungrily through the stacks of vast libraries filled with frustration that he cannot read and possess all of those books. As a graduate student of English, I must have been one of the few members of the class in "Introduction to Library Studies"—or whatever it was called—who enjoyed learning how to find his way through the labyrinth of a major research library like Illinois'. All of those bibliographies of bibliographies inspired awe.

And I got some sense of the history of the campus, as well, when I spent my afternoons for several months in the basement University Archives, paging through one hundred years of the *Daily Illini* while writing an informal history of undergraduate life on the campus. The university was observing its centennial and this project was conceived as a sort of footnote to the official history; I'm not sure what significance can be attached to a 1925 classified ad in which Red Grange offered his Ford for sale ("Goes like 60"), but there was a thrill of discovery in finding it.

My favorite library room was at the University of Cape Town, where I had a fellowship for a year of graduate study. The English graduate students' seminar was a big, old, wood-paneled room lined with complete sets of the classics and the basic English authors, and the bay windows stood open in nice weather so that the vines blew in and the view was clear down the slopes of Table Mountain while I read (somewhat distractedly, under the conditions) *Confessions of an English Opium Eater*, or some such. There's nothing quite like the romance of a good library with its seemingly infinite reaches of volumes and its ultimate promise: the good book not yet read.

The library I use most often these days is the *Chicago Sun-Times/Daily News* library, a large and awe-inspiring room just across the hall from the city rooms of the two newspapers. It's named the "library" in big, bold letters on the door, and that's the way the guides describe it to people taking a tour of the building; but in my heart I nurse a sneaky affection for the old-fashioned term "morgue." Not only are the clips on lots of dead (and living) newsmakers buried there, but so are the facts about thousands of old movies.

I get a lot of calls from readers who want to know when Gary Cooper died, or whether Elizabeth Taylor was in "Jane Eyre" (she was, in an uncredited cameo), or how many actors played Tarzan, or whether Maximillian Schell and Maria Schell are brother and sister. The answers to most of these questions are in Leslie Halliwell's invaluable *The Filmgoer's Companion* (New York: Hill & Wang, 1974), which just went into its fourth revised edition. Casts and credits for almost all movies since 1950 can be found in Crown's *Screen World* series, and Quigley's *International Motion Picture Almanac*, badly dated and incomplete for several years, but just revised and reset in a new format.

There are more esoteric sources for movie data and trivia, too, of which the most ambitious and interesting is Ernest Parmentier's *Filmfacts*. This is an indispensable and in many ways amazing compilation of almost everything you'd ever want to read about current movies. It's issued every other week in a magazine format ranging from twenty-eight to sixty closely packed pages, and it attempts to deal with every single film, no matter how humble, obscure, or totally worthless, that opened commercially in the United States during the year.

Filmfacts provides the complete cast (down to the smallest walk-on); all of the credits (even, to take an example from *Last Tango in Paris*, the name of the musician who performed the saxaphone solo); a synopsis of the plot; a summary of the general critical reception; and then reprints of three to five complete reviews from major magazines and newspapers in New York, Chicago,

Los Angeles, and Washington. This labor of love and great industry perennially falls behind; a desperate Parmentier skipped 1970 entirely in an attempt to catch up (promising to get back to it later), and is currently in the midst of 1973. Still, *Filmfacts* is the most reliable and complete source of film facts there is.

Our library also contains the gargantuan volumes reprinting all of the *New York Times* film reviews; the index to this set provides a reliable guide to, among other things, the correct spelling of the names of almost anyone who ever had anything to do with movies. For films considered to be serious, artistic, or historically significant, George Sadoul's *Dictionary of Films* and *Dictionary of Filmmakers* (both Berkeley: Univ. of California Pr., 1972) provide concise information (including a digest of each film's key scenes). And then there are our clips themselves, row upon row of envelopes containing yellowing reviews, interviews, think pieces, still photos, and sometimes even old programs.

Dead center of the *Sun-Times/Daily News* library is currently occupied by a very large, inscrutable, vaguely intimidating book of computer gear that somewhat resembles the monolith in *2001: A Space Odyssey*. Our chief librarian promises that before long all of those old clippings will be magically spirited into the innards of this device, to be preserved on microfilm. Our newspapers are run as sound business enterprises, and I assume that large amounts of money would not have been spent on the monolith if this were not so; still, the beast still squats there in the middle of the floor, the clippings still come in brown envelopes, and computer experts circle their offspring warily, scratching their heads and hefting their screwdrivers.

For all their virtues, however, libraries don't yet take feature films as seriously as I would like (or, in some cases, even really consider them part of what a library should include in its basic collection). Film is a nuisance, I know. Prints are expensive or impossible to obtain.

Storage is a problem. In-library projection facilities cost money and take space and can serve only a fraction of the users that the same space could accommodate in readers. When films are loaned out, there's the problem of whom they'll be shown to, and whether appropriate conditions of exhibition will be met.

And yet any library which prides itself on offering the important authors should also, I believe, eventually hope to offer the basic directors, as well: John Ford as well as Hemingway, Fellini as well as Moravia, Bergman as well as Ibsen, Renoir as well as Camus. Perhaps cassettes and videotapes will eventually become inexpensive and portable enough to provide the answer. I hope so. Meanwhile libraries show educational films and sometimes experimental films. They supply the books that make a viewer film-literate. As someone who has cast his lot with movies (while still reading about as much as ever), I'd like to think that libraries will continue to expand so that for the young library user and borrower of ten or twenty years from now, the library will be equally a source of cinematic adventure.

George Plimpton

THE PLIMPTON SMALL BALL THEORY

Query: I understand you have a theory about the relative value of sports books.

Answer: Well, it's not a terribly serious method of evaluation . . . but it has occurred to me that in books about sports in which a ball is used, there is an odd correlation between the size of the ball and the value of the literary work about whatever sport is involved: the smaller the ball, the better the book.

Q.: You are suggesting that there have been few essential and brilliant books on medicine balls.

A.: Exactly.

Q.: Or on beach balls, and sports involving them?

A.: You've got the point. Absolutely.

Q.: So a book about . . .

A.: "Stick to the small spheroids for good reading," is my maxim of the moment. For example, golf has an extraordinary output of first-rate books. Even the players seem to write decently about what they do. The best account is Robert Jones's *Golf Is My Game*, which he wrote himself (a rarity indeed from a sports figure) with a skill comparable to his abilities with a golf stick. As for the nonplayers, the list is long. The finest of the contemporary golf writers is Herbert Warren Wind. He has been compared to Robert Surtees and quite aptly. The best of his books is entitled (rather grandly) *Herbert Warren Wind's Golf Book*. The moxie of putting his name ahead of the sport he writes about is okay by me. Now, as you know, the British golf ball is smaller than ours, and here the Plimpton maxim seems to work—surely the finest books about golf are by Bernard Darwin, the grandson of the great naturalist. He was trained for the law but felt he was "throwing his life away" practicing it; so in 1908 he gave up the law and wrote golf pieces for the *Times* for forty-five years. These are collected in books—*Playing the Like*, *Out of the Rough*, *Green Memories*—and they are all splendid. P. G. Wodehouse's books on golf (it would be hard to write serious fiction about such an infuriating game) are the best, and the best of them is *Divots*. My favorite of all golf books is the *Golfer's Handbook* (British published, of course, although there is an American abridgement), which is an almanac about the sport that must be read to be believed.

Q.: Could we talk about larger balls . . .

A.: Baseballs! Next up the scale. Probably the two best novels about sports are baseball books—Mark Harris's *The Southpaw* and *Bang the Drum Slowly*. He has written a third novel about the same characters, but I have not read it, thinking it might hurt my wonder at the first two. I've even forgotten its name.* The first two are classics. I've never been especially easy with Ring Lardner's "classic" *You Know Me, Al* or with *Lose with a Smile*, its sequel, perhaps because of the epistolary device Lardner uses. Of course, "Alibi Ike," out of the first volume, is, along with James Thurber's "You Could Look It Up," a great short sports classic. The two best books by players are Jim Brosnan's *The Long Season* (he wrote it himself) and Jim Bouton's controversial *Ball Four* (with which he had editorial help from Leonard Shecter). Both books are puckish and funny and illuminating, especially the former. Two excellent nonfiction accounts that crept onto best-seller lists (which is a rare place for any sports book) are Roger Angell's *The Summer Game* and Roger Kahn's *The Boys of Summer*. Angell's is the more enterprising, being a superbly written personal study of the game, whereas Kahn relied largely on interviews with ancient Brooklyn Dodgers, much in line with the practice used by Lawrence Ritter in his excellent book of interviews with old-timers, entitled *The Glory of Their Times*.

Q.: It occurs to me that a tennis ball is about the same size as a baseball.

A.: Lighter, obviously. Not as much density. John McPhee has written the best book I've read on the sport so far: *Levels of the Game*, which is about the thought processes running through the minds of two players, Arthur Ashe and Clark Graebner, as they play a match at Forest Hills. More recently, McPhee has done a study

***A Ticket for a Seamstitch*, published in 1957 and long since out of print.

of Wimbledon, which indeed is called that: *Wimbledon, A Celebration.* The best book I've read by a player is Rod Laver's *The Education of a Tennis Player*, on which he was helped by Bud Collins.

Q.: Well, football is enormously popular these days. It employs a relatively large ball.

A.: And so its literature offers very slim pickings. I don't know why. Perhaps it's because the ball is not only large but misshapen. The best survey of the sport itself if a somewhat technical view, is a book by Paul Zimmerman entitled *A Thinking Man's Guide to Pro Football.* The best of the player's as-told-to variety is Jerry Kramer's *Instant Replay*, about a season with the Green Bay Packers. Others in the nonfiction pack would include Vince Lombardi's and W. C. Heinz's *Run to Daylight*, which is a study of Lombardi's preparation of the Green Bay Packers for an important game against opponents whom Lombardi refuses to identify (they are in fact the Detroit Lions), which is too bad since the opposition becomes noncorporeal, rather as if the game were being played by phone, like a transatlantic chess match. Still, a fine study. Also, I am fond of Myron Cope's collection of reminiscences by old-time football players, *The Game That Was*, perhaps not as interesting as Ritter's *The Glory of Their Times*, but with great sections nonetheless. I have not yet read a novel about football in which the game either served the characters properly or was illuminated by the characters. If one is interested in vigorous attempts, he should look into Frederick Exley's *A Fan's Notes*, Don DeLillo's *End Zone*, and more recently, Dan Jenkins's *Semi-Tough* and Pete Gent's *North Dallas Forty*.

Q.: If the fault of football novels is, as you suggest, that the ball is misshapen and bounces crazily, what about basketball?

A.: That ball must be too big. The reading is slim. John McPhee (again!) wrote a study of Bill Bradley at Princeton entitled *A Sense of Where You Are*, which is certainly the best I've read so far. Bill Bradley tells me that he is writing a book himself . . . so we have that to look forward to. I have not yet read David Wolf's *Foul: The Connie Hawkins Story*, but I am told on good authority that it is essential. John Updike's *Rabbit Run* I have ruled out on the ground that metaphorical basketballs escape all other standards of measurement.

Q.: What about major sports in which a ball is not used? Boxing, for instance.

A.: Another corollary, and a far less frivolous one than the Plimpton Small Ball Theory, is that the more dangerous the confrontation in a sport, the more interesting its literature. The superb books on exploration, mountain climbing, big-game hunting—all of which put men under considerable stress—would make an endless list. To soothe those who detest bullfighting, or consider it an art, not a sport, we'll leave out what would have been an interesting selection. Boxing, which really puts a man up against it, even if the opposition is a mirror of himself, offers a strong literature—beginning with the great essays of Pierce Egan. The best contemporary list would include John Lardner's *Great White Hopes and Other Tigers* and A. J. Liebling's *The Sweet Science.* The fights and fighters the two writers describe are long gone, but how splendidly they are brought to life! Everything that Norman Mailer has written about boxing should be read, though unfortunately his essays on the topic have been scattered among his nonfiction collections. The exception is his account of the Frazier/Ali fight, *King of the Hill.* A publisher would do well to bring out a separate volume. The best novels are Budd Schulberg's *The Harder They Fall* and a novel by W. C. Heinz entitled *The Professional,* though the ending of the latter is so shattering that it's impossible to read the book twice.

Q.: What about auto racing? That's surely a dangerous sport?

A.: Certainly. And correspondingly, its literature is superb, and, if I may say so, neglected by sports enthusiasts. Among the best racing books are two by Robert Daley, the same gent who recently quit his job as Deputy Police Commissioner for Public Affairs of New York City—*Cars at Speed* and *The Cruel Sport.* I also admire a book by the great British racing driver Stirling Moss, entitled *All But My Life.* And lastly, an absolutely first-rate diary called *Faster!* by Jackie Stewart, last year's international driving champion. These would be representative. May I mention anthologies?

Q.: Certainly.

A.: It's worth mentioning anthologies, because the best sport pieces are so often short, or descriptive, or analytical pieces that don't turn into books. The two best I know are Herbert Warren Wind's (again!) *The Realm of Sport* and a collection by Paul Gallico of his own pieces entitled *Farewell to Sport.*

Q.: Some of the books you mentioned are out of print and only a few book stores carry a full stock of sports books. Finding an elusive book can be a sport in itself, can't it?

A.: That's right, but even an amateur book-finder has good odds on finding the book he wants at his public library and here you can reverse the small ball theory. The bigger the library the better. But even a small library can hunt down an elusive title through interlibrary loan.

William Cole

A SEMI-LIBRARIAN

One day a year ago, on upper Times Square, near where I live, I came across a young woman I know on her way to work. Not a particularly unusual occurrence, except that in this case she was totally absorbed in a paperback, oblivious to the hurrying crowds on the sidewalk. "Jane!" I shouted, "Admirable! Admirable!" interrupting her in the middle of her Dostoyevsky. Why the fuss? she wanted to know, and I explained that you just don't *see* anybody doing that sort of thing anymore. People don't walk along the street reading. At least not where I live. The episode took me back to the time in the mid-thirties when I became a reader. I was brought up in a New York suburb, and I remember, in my early teens, walking a mile-and-a-half to the library a couple of times a week, taking out the maximum number of books—I believe it was six—and walking the mile-and-a-half back home, reading all the way. I seem to recall walking in the gutter, and logic tells me that, walking that way, I wouldn't be constantly interrupted by having to step down and up curbs at the cross streets. Not so many cars in those days.

My reading afoot was not, sorry to say, Dostoyevsky, but more likely Rider Haggard, John Buchan, P. G. Wodehouse, or Mazo de la Roche with whom I had a short-lived but intense literary affair, whipping through the three hundred—is it?—*Jalna* books in a swoop. That suburb had a fine public library, and I recall the pleasure of graduating from the children's room to the adult —a sort of Christian bar mitzvah. On that occasion the librarian kindly asked me what I wanted for my first adult book. Shy, I mumbled, "A sea story." She didn't quite hear, saying, "Oh, a mystery story!" and disappeared in the stacks, emerging with a book that wasn't a mystery story, but which I dutifully read all the way through. It was in that same library, in the magazine room, that I was first introduced to the glorious mysteries of the female body, through the kindly pages of the *National Geographic*. Librarians, and millions of ex-boys, will know what I mean.

Later, in another suburb, I decided to educate myself, to put down a base. A magazine featured Somerset Maugham's list of twenty-five books every educated man should read; the library had all of them, and I plowed my way through, and emerged, months later, educated, save for no knowledge whatsoever of languages, philosophy, religion, mathematics, geology, economics, bee culture, or feminine psychology.

Then, in connection with the late war, the post library at Camp Livingston, Louisiana, was my next hangout. I was editing a mimeographed regimental newspaper and used the library—it was well-stocked, and all the books were pristine—to research a series of articles about great humorists—a series that I'm sure baffled my fellow-soldiers, but pleased me immensely. I also sat in for the librarian from time to time, and learned Mr. Dewey's system. Shortly thereafter, at a sultry camp on the Florida coast, and at another sweltering one near Richmond, Virginia, I built up a regimental library of a couple of thousand scruffy books rounded up from helpful citizens, and established myself in a large, dank tent which doubled as the publishing office for my paper. It was also the goof-off place for myself and my friends to take naps, so it served a triple morale purpose. When we moved overseas from Richmond, I found an immense wooden crate, easily the size of four coffins, and convinced the officer in charge that the library had to move with us. I well remember the terrible time eight husky soldiers had moving that box, and a dozen others, onto a truck, and the murderous looks they gave me, the librarian.

Once in Europe, the giant box and its companions mysteriously disappeared for eight months while we were stationed in a Welsh castle, but just as mysteriously reappeared when we moved to an encampment on Salisbury Plain. There I once again persuaded those in charge to let me run a library, and I set up the books in a ramshackle tin building placed oddly in the middle of a sort of parade ground, and I further managed to get permission to sleep in the building to avoid theft. (The only book ever stolen was Waugh's *Vile Bodies*—and surely for the wrong reasons.) My fellow soldiers slept in cramped tents on the periphery of the parade ground, and every morning they were aroused at six to do calisthenics and police the area—pick up cigarette butts and other small debris. I got the feeling that they resented my library when they started kicking the reverberating sides of my building on their policing missions, snarling things like "Lazy bum!" and "Wake up, Cole!"

There were about fifty worthwhile books in the library—some Graham Greene, Wodehouse, Waugh, Mencken, Hemingway, and a few poetry anthologies—these I kept in circulation, pressing them on the sometimes unwilling customers. Truly a "personal" librarian. We moved to France a week after D day, leaving my library to who knows what fate. Then, immediately after the war ended, I was stationed in Germany, and the question came up, "Would you like to go to library school in Paris for two weeks?" Hah! Would I? And I, a mere corporal, was given a jeep and driver and sent off. There was no library, mind you, nor none in prospect, but somebody higher up had decided that the army just might need some semilibrarians sometime in the future, so I found myself one of fifty happy soldiers attending classes at Cité Université, learning how to alphabetize, which is about all that was taught. But we did have a fascinating afternoon with Gertrude Stein and—need it be said—Alice B. Toklas. I remember looking out the window and seeing Gertrude and Alice sitting majestically in the back seat of a jeep drawing into the courtyard. I can't remember a thing Stein said, but she was a riveting presence. Alice Toklas sat quietly knitting throughout in the last seat in the classroom.

My two weeks training taught nothing I hadn't known before, and it probably cost the army a couple of thousand dollars. But it was worth it to me. Later, at a dispersal camp, or whatever they were called, I did a brief stint as a librarian, but the soldiers were too distracted by thoughts of going home, and nobody paid much attention to the library.

Being an anthologist, my working life involves libraries deeply, and I've practically lived in libraries on and off for the past twenty years. I can usually be found crouched down in a child's chair in the children's room, reading poetry. And I spend a good deal of time at library card indexes. Any time I'm in a strange town, with a moment to spare, I drop in to the local library and count how many anthologies I have in the collection. Gives a man a fine feeling to know that he has six books in the Stockbridge, Massachusetts, collection, twelve in East Hampton, New York, and seven in a Tucson branch library. Discouraging though to find another man with exactly the same name who wrote a book on diet popping up in the midst of your cards! But the cards are there, and it's nice to know that you've done some books that librarians feel "fill that hole in the library shelf."

And no, I don't read on the street. On subways and buses, in waiting rooms, and, the sure sign of a city reader, in elevators and on escalators, cannily judging beforehand whether the ride will be long enough to warrant whipping out the reading glasses, finding my place in the book, reading a paragraph, and replacing the glasses.

Clara S. Jones

EPILOGUE

If most people were asked to select the one institution in the community that is absolutely basic, the choice would be an impossible one because all our institutions are needed to serve our many different needs. However, if pressed to make a single selection, many would choose hospitals, the police force, or perhaps the more philosophical would name the church or the public school. On first thought the public library would hardly be included in any group of indispensable institutions. But let us examine the library's place in society. Ancient pictures on the walls of caves reveal that almost from the beginning of time human beings attempted to record their history and way of life. As writing developed they recorded their discoveries about the physical world and their thoughts about themselves and each other on the leaves of the papyrus plant, which was the earliest form of paper. These were actually the first libraries—the walls of caves and the papyrus scrolls. If the ability to write and read had not been developed, and if the records had not been preserved for posterity, civilization as we know it could never have evolved. In other words, if every generation had to transmit by word of mouth all it had learned about survival and mastering the natural environment, progress in technology would still be in its infancy. Today, every manufacturing plant, business, or governmental agency depends for its existence on the printed word and on having recorded knowledge organized into specialized fields. To gather this world of information, to organize and preserve it and make it readily available, is the function of a library. Every institution rests squarely on this base provided by libraries.

The popular impression that libraries are only for a restricted few should be discarded. Because under past segregation practices few public libraries were open to black patrons, library use has not played a historic role in the lives of most black people. However, the civil rights movement of the sixties and seventies removed barriers to the use of governmental agencies, and public libraries have changed with the times. They have responded to the interests and needs of black citizens of all ages by offering a wide variety of books, magazines, films, and phonograph records on Afro-American history and culture. Black librarians are hired at all levels and serve in all parts of library systems. Furthermore, the public libraries of the nation have mounted a giant-sized campaign to provide programs that are relative to the needs of the many different kinds of people they serve. Librarians' skills and inventiveness know no bounds and the resulting imaginative programming has benefitted the entire population. There are highly interesting programs for every age, taste, interest, and background. Certainly libraries feature the role that black people have played in the development of the nation. Afro-American History Week programs are the most prominent of all the ethnic programs in the public library.

Public libraries are designed to serve not only all kinds of interests and needs, but both readers and nonreaders. A children's storybook, a novel for adults, or an account of an adventurous journey to a faraway place are read from cover to cover by the confirmed "reader." On the other hand, a person who borrows a book from the library on auto repair does not sit in an armchair and "read" that book. When it is returned it might very well have a black thumbprint or a faint trace of grease on the pages. Technically, this patron is a "nonreader" because the book was not read in the usual sense. It was *used* for a very practical purpose. The person probably placed the open book on the fender of his car while he worked on the motor, turning the pages as he needed specific steps in the process of making repairs. This same kind of use is made by the person who wishes to convert a basement into a recreation room. Books and magazines are *used* for ideas and suggestions on home decoration and color schemes, on carpentry, laying carpet, and so forth. The "user" might also be a "reader," but many who are strictly "users" patronize libraries regularly because, like the "readers," they have discovered that an infinite number of their interests can be satisfied by the library. There are still others who are characteristically "nonreaders," who never thought of going into a library until, for example, they applied for civil service positions or wished to take promotional examinations in the skilled trades. At this point they learned that the public library provides practice tests and they made their first library visit to borrow them in order to prepare for the examination. These may be one-time library patrons, but their pressing needs have been met. Having made the discovery of the practical service of the library, this initial visit sometimes serves as an introduction to other books and library materials, and many become library "users" or "readers."

We take information for granted in our daily lives, but if we stop to think about it, the mastery of information actually determines our status in life. In learning a skilled trade, preparing for a career in science or the arts, or any vocation, we are mastering specialized information that will enable us to earn a living and develop our individual talents. The more limited our store of information the more restricted our capability in attaining the necessities, comforts, and pleasures on which to build the "good life." In our everyday lives, problems and questions arise that require specific information for solution.

In today's society there is a vast complex of offices, organizations, and institutions to be dealt with in connection with our personal lives, families, and jobs. People are shunted about from one telephone number to another, from one agency to another, to the point of discouragement and despair. Help is actually available for nearly all our problems, but the efforts of many who seek help are too often thwarted in the maze. Until recently there was no one central starting point where needed information could be attained or direct guidance to the proper source given. The public library is now developing into this needed, general community information center. It can supply answers to everyday, life-size questions of all kinds, or refer the inquirer to the source he or she needs. In very recent years librarians have gone out into their communities to gather nonbook information on every aspect of life and service. They have organized this information into files that now give a very complete picture of what a community is like and what services it offers its residents. Information and referral service is an important arm of public library work. It is actually reference work in the community, employing the same time-honored techniques as reference work in books and other printed sources. Public response has been very enthusiastic, especially by telephone. Every public library system gives its own special name to its information and referral service, but everywhere it means the use of the public library as the first-stop, neighborhood information center that either gives the desired information or directs the person to its source. If the public library ever seemed remote and unrelated to real life, this is no longer true.

It is children who constitute the largest body of public library patrons. A librarian from the nearest branch library visiting school classrooms to tell stories is like the "Pied Piper of Hamelin" who played his pipe and lured all the children away—only in this instance they hasten to the library for more good stories. All the world loves a story—romance, mysteries, high adventure, tall tales, or true life stories. Even the nursery rhymes that very small children enjoy contain a suggestion of a story. Children who have someone to read to them at a very early age start acquiring a larger vocabulary; they learn to listen and concentrate, and their horizons are broadened beyond the time and place where they live and the people they know. Their curiosity and interest stimulate them to learn more about people, places, and things. They associate pleasure with books and reading. The day a small child is brought to the library for his or her first library card is a day filled with keen anticipation of the wonders that will unfold in the world of books. As these children progress in school, learning to read, they will have far more than the minimum practice and drill that are so necessary in mastering the mechanics of reading and spelling. Early in the school career there will be a great contrast between these pupils and the child who has never had the joy of having someone read to him or her, and who experiences only the reading practice provided in the classroom. Practice is necessary to make a good reader, just as to make a good athlete. Children's speaking vocabularies far exceed their reading vocabularies; therefore, they can enjoy hearing many stories that they would not be able to read for themselves for several years to come. Just as important is the fact that motivation to learn has been implanted in the children who have learned to love stories and books early in life. A good student is necessarily a willing student because requirements and force are no match for self-motivation.

At every grade level, use of the library plays an important role because the children who read beyond the classroom are able to gain more from instruction. They actually know more in all areas than those who read only the minimum school requirements. The habitual readers express themselves well, and the excellence of their performance gives them self-confidence and poise, and inspires the confidence and respect of others in their ability. Therefore, they are the ones nominated by their peers or called upon by their teachers to represent the class or participate in school functions, thus giving them additional experiences. Their broad reading takes them on magic carpets to all parts of the world, and back and forth into all periods of history. Without realizing it, through their reading these children are learning to be at home on the earth, accustomed to the differences in people and ways of life and outlook. It is natural for them to find the variety in human life interesting, not frightening or repulsive. When they graduate from high school, their learning experience will obviously have been far richer than that of the children whose awareness and knowledge have been more restricted.

Programs for children of all ages are an important part of branch library service. Delightful preschool story hours are offered in weekly series. Stories, rhymes, picture books, and singing games are planned, usually for three- and four-year-olds. Mothers commonly report that their children will not let them miss their weekly library program. Time is well spent in providing this activity because small children are eager and responsive. When parents bring their children to the story hour they have the opportunity to browse in the adult collection for themselves and also to become acquainted with the kinds of books children enjoy. Librarians give guidance in the selection of stories to read to children and of gifts to purchase for them. If this early acquaintance with books is fortified by reading to children at home plus the later use of the library, the children will be well on their way to becoming book lovers for life. Indeed, the love of books and reading can be an important factor in the rearing of children, helping them to enjoy the exercise of their own minds.

Librarians have extended themselves deeply into the community. They attend community meetings and participate actively, taking advantage of every opportunity to put up displays and distribute book lists. Organizations are encouraged to hold meetings in library buildings whenever possible. Most churches have graciously welcomed librarians at their regular services as well as in their special groups. Librarians are available to speak at all types of community meetings and are frequently called upon to give book reviews.

There exists in some places a persistent but unreal notion that although public libraries are good to have, they have little meaning for most people. However, the person in the street as well as the community leader or bureaucrat can discover the truly meaningful role of the public library in their lives, as many of the essays in this book have shown. A whole new world opens with the discovery that this "peoples' university" and community information center offers everyday life-giving service, opening doors to self-development and the continuing realization of human potential.

Author Biographies

JACOB K. JAVITS

Jacob K. Javits, now serving in the United States Senate from the state of New York, is also a trial lawyer. He has served with distinction on the many Senate committees to which he has been appointed, and has lectured and written on both economic and political subjects.

MARCHETTE CHUTE

Marchette Chute has to her credit an extensive list of titles. She graduated with a bachelor of arts, magna cum laude, from the University of Minnesota. She holds three honorary degrees as a doctor of letters and is a member of Phi Beta Kappa and of the American Academy of Arts and Letters. She has received various awards, including the Constance Lindsay Skinner Award for service to books.

NAT IRVING HENTOFF

Nat Irving Hentoff, whose career experiences have included those of writer, producer, music adviser, columnist, and author, is also a well-known civil libertarian. He is a lover of jazz and is the co-editor of the *Jazz Review* and a staff writer for the *New Yorker*.

EZRA JACK KEATS

Ezra Jack Keats is a respected author-illustrator who has received numerous honors, awards, and citations during his career of illustrating and writing children's books, many of which now appear in ten languages. *The Snowy Day* won the Caldecott Medal in 1963; *Goggles!* was a Caldecott Honor Book in 1970; *Hi, Cat!* received the Boston Globe-Horn Book Award in 1970; and *The Snowy Day* was included in the State Department's exhibition of graphic arts which toured the Soviet Union.

SOL YURICK

Sol Yurick is a novelist and short story writer. He regularly contributes to literary journals, and is the author of *The Bag*, *Fertig*, and *Someone Just Like You*.

HERMAN BADILLO

Herman Badillo is an attorney and former New York congressman from the twenty-first district. He served with distinction on many congressional committees and was especially interested in prison reform. His two books, *A Bill of No Rights* and *Attica and the American Prison System*, underscore this interest.

ELTON C. FAX

Elton C. Fax is an illustrator who has combined artistic talent and literary skill. He has illustrated almost thirty children's books and has authored six books, mostly for adults and dealing with black artists. He studied drawing and painting at Syracuse University and has received awards for both his artistic and literary efforts.

CAROLINE BIRD

Caroline Bird has written extensively regarding the economic problems and opportunities of women. She has been a member of the editorial staffs of *Fortune*, *Newsweek*, and the *New York Journal of Commerce*; and has herself written over two hundred magazine articles on economic and sociological subjects.

LAVINIA RUSS

Lavinia Russ is an authority on children's books. She has been a buyer of children's books for Scribner's book store, children's book editor for *Publishers Weekly*, and co-producer of a television program entitled "Children Explore Books." Lavinia Russ has four titles to her credit: *Over the Hills and Far Away*, *Alec's Sand Castle*, *The April Age*, and *A Young Explorer's New York* (written under the name of Lavinia Faxon). Now retired, she gives of her time by reading to the children at St. Luke's School in New York.

NORMAN COUSINS

Norman Cousins is the editor of the *Saturday Review* and has served in editorial capacities elsewhere. He has written many books which pertain to foreign affairs, has been honored for his journalistic achievements, and has received recognition for his numerous efforts in public service.

JOSETTE FRANK

Josette Frank is a leading early childhood educator. She has been on the staff of the Child Study Association of America/Wel-Met Inc. for many years, where she is director for Children's Books and Mass Media. She also serves on the book selection committee of the National Conference of Christians and Jews. She has written two books, *What Books for Children?* and *Your Child's Reading Today*, and two pamphlets, *Television: How to Use It Wisely with Children* and *Comics, T.V., Radio and Movies—What Do They Offer Children?*

DOROTHY RODGERS

Dorothy Rodgers possesses diverse talents. She is a sculptor and designer, inventor of marketable products, and a writer. She has written three books: *My Favorite Things, The House in My Head*, and *A Word to the Wives*. She has also co-authored a monthly column for a women's magazine and co-hosted a radio program.

R. A. CLEM LABINE

Clem Labine, a chemical engineer noteworthy for his editorial accomplishments and whose hobby is restoration of old homes, is currently editor of the *Old-House Journal*, a monthly publication devoted to the restoration of pre-1914 houses. Mr. Labine was with McGraw-Hill for fifteen years before starting his *Journal*. As hinted in his essay, he is slowly restoring his 1883 brownstone to its original Victorian elegance.

VARTANIG G. VARTAN

Vartanig G. Vartan is a leading financial writer. He has been with the *New York Times* for fourteen years and previously wrote a column for the *New York Herald Tribune*. His newspaper career began in 1948 when, after graduating from Yale University, he served as a reporter for various small daily papers in Mississippi.

ROGER EBERT

Roger Ebert is the film critic of the *Chicago Sun-Times.* His talents are demonstrated in his varied careers as writer, instructor of English, and lecturer. His film reviews have been recognized by various awards.

GEORGE PLIMPTON

George Plimpton is an author who has an insatiable zest for life. His extraordinary experiences range from being an instructor at Barnard College, to serving in various editorial capacities for *Horizon* and *Sports Illustrated,* to being an active participant in the sports about which he has written.

WILLIAM COLE

William Cole, whose formal education did not extend beyond high school, has established himself as a generalist of the book publishing world. He has to his credit fifty anthologies in the fields of poetry, humor, cartoons, and folk songs. He has his own publishing imprint, "William Cole Books," with the Viking Press and has for the past two years written the "Trade Winds" column for the *Saturday Review.*

CLARA STANTON JONES

Clara Stanton Jones is a librarian of extraordinary breadth and competence, who is serving as Director of the Detroit Public Library where her career dates back to 1944. She was president of the American Library Association for 1976/77. Her activities are centered in Detroit and concentrate on the revitalization and cultural development of that city. Mrs. Jones is well known in the Detroit community and articles by and about her have appeared in numerous journals. She holds memberships in various professional and cultural associations and she has been the recipient of several honorary degrees.